Korean-American Voices of Youth in New Jersey

Korean-American Voices of Youth in New Jersey

Edited by

Esther Hah

The Hermit Kingdom Press
Highland Park * Seoul * Bangalore * Cebu

Korean-American Voices of Youth in New Jersey

Hardcover ISBN13: 978-1-59689-074-9
Paperback ISBN13: 978-1-59689-075-6

Write To Address:
The Hermit Kingdom Press
P. O. Box 1226
Highland Park, NJ 08904-1226
The United States of America

United States Library of Congress Control Number: 2007943829

Table of Contents

Preface . . . . p. 1

"The Birmingham Dream: An Inspirational Story of Hardship, Friendship, and a Fight for Equality" /Joe Kim/ . . . . p. 5

"Korean Americans vs. African Americans" /Brian Lee/ . . . . p. 60

"My Church Called the Praise Church" /Brian Kim/ . . . . p. 68

"Emancipation to Benefit the White Man" /John Baek/ . . . p. 72

"Educational Problems in Korea in Light of Korean History" /Paul Park/ . . . . p. 80

"Uncle Tom's Cabin and Koreans" /David Lee/ . . . . p. 90

"Tradition and Lottery" /Joon Park/ . . . . p. 94

"What I Think Korea Is Like" /Gloria Bae/ . . . . p. 97

"My Korean-American Journey" /Esther Hah/ . . . . p. 100

Preface

It gives me great pleasure to be the editor of the volume, *Korean-American Voices of Youth in New Jersey*, and have the opportunity to collect sundry voices of Korean Americans from all over New Jersey. There are over 2 million Korean Americans in the U.S and many of them come from different backgrounds from South Korea, and some have been in America for three generations. Often, Korean Americans who live in one region wonder if all Korean Americans are similar throughout the U.S, especially for Korean American teenagers whose lives are confined to their high schools and their families, the curiosity regarding other Korean Americans is great. In this volume, I would like to present the voices of Korean American in New Jersey and provide a picture of what it is like to be a Korean American teenager in NJ.

I would imagine that Korean Americans are quite similar throughout the U.S because what unites us is greater than what separates us. All Korean Americans speak the Korean language, even though some may speak a very limited version of it. A part of the reason that necessitates speaking the Korean language is the fact that the majority of the parents speak predominantly or exclusively the Korean language at home. Even the Korean parents who speak the English language rather fluently would prefer to speak to their children in Korean because they do not feel as comfortable speaking in English as the Korean language is a commonality among Americans in America is further cemented in the institution of the Korean Church. From Los Angeles to New Jersey, most Korean Christians attend Korean American Churches. Every American who has driven by an "American" church has probably seen signs in Korean announcing Korean American services after American congregations finish theirs in the morning. Korean American churches predominantly conduct their services in Korean, and the leadership generally speaks exclusively in Korean. There are youth services, generally held in English, but they are relatively a small part of the Korean Church, around 10-20% of the church membership. The rest speak Korean and attend Korean services. This phenomenon has not changed despite the fact that Korean immigration to America is over 100 years old.

Korean culture is an important part of Korean Americans. This is not only the case for first Korean generation, but also the case for Korean American youth. That is why it should not be surprising that when people go to schools with a large number of Korean Americans, they will see Korean Americans associating generally amongst themselves. Korean American teens gravitate toward other Korean Americans. Those Koreans who attend high schools that do not have many Korean Americans usually spend most of their weekends at the Korean American church where they can enjoy companionship with other Korean Americans with whom they can identify with rather than with their non-Korean friends in their high schools.

Many non-Korean Americans frankly do not understand the need for Korean Americans to bond with each other and often they complaint that Korean Americans segregate themselves. I do not believe that is the most constructive way to look at Korean American friendships. It is not a question about segregation or assimilation. It is a question of people who feel a commonality bonding around that commonality. It is not different from Southerners gravitating toward Southerners in a setting that includes people from all over the country. It is not different from people who went to same colleges who bond with those who went to the same college at alumni meetings and social programs.

I hope that this book will offer Koreans and non-Koreans alike a picture of the feelings, experiences, and world views about Korean Americans in New Jersey. I also hope that this book will be a source that provides greater understanding of Koreans for non-Koreans. And I hope that for Korean Americans throughout the country that this book will provide a view into a segment of their fellow Korean Americans from the state of New Jersey and help them better understand themselves.

Esther Hah
Closter, NJ
2007

"The Birmingham Dream: An Inspirational Story of Hardship, Friendship, and a Fight for Equality"

By Joe Kim (11th Grade, Lincroft, NJ)

"Nonviolence is the answer to the crucial political and moral questions of our time; the need for mankind to overcome oppression and violence without resorting to oppression and violence. Mankind must evolve for all human conflict a method which rejects revenge, aggression, and retaliation. The foundation of such a method is love." Martin Luther King, Jr.

Introduction

People all around the world dub America as, "The Land of Equality," and "A Nation Full of Opportunities." As a Korean high school student living here, I realize every day that inter-ethnic conflicts still exist, today. Probably the most influential case was during the mid-1900's between the African-Americans and the White-Americans. From the infamous case, *Brown vs. Board of Education*, to the Montgomery Bus Boycott, which was sparked by an average Black woman by the name of Rosa Parks who refused to give up her seat on a bus to a White man, it was evident that America wasn't living up to its recognition. For a span of almost 15 years, the racial discrimination towards the African-Americans in the South caused outrage between the two parties, as it was fairly rare to see people of mixed race mingle with one another. I was inspired to write this story after watching my favorite film of all-time, "Remember the Titans." If unfamiliar with the movie, it depicts a Virginia high school that was just newly integrated from three different schools. The high school football team, mixed with both Blacks and Whites, were able to set aside their prejudices and overcome obstacles to respect one another and win championships together. By helping their community to also put aside their intolerance and join together, the Virginia high school and its story truly dug into my heart. At the time I finished watching this film, which was when I was about 10 years old, I actually then showed "Remember the Titans" to my parents. My parents were born in Korea and immigrated here in 1986, so they were obviously unfamiliar with our country's past. I was pleasantly astonished by how quickly they were able to grasp the significance of the story, mainly because they and their fellow Koreans had rarely experienced any sort of hostility in their homeland. (My mom was only familiar with the South Los Angeles incidents between Korean merchants and Black customers from the newspaper, which I won't get into.)

My goal in writing this story is to mainly target young teenagers (barring the language in the novel) to try to teach them about the ongoing aversion that holds a place in every person's heart in this country. It is very disturbing to listen to and watch people on television yell obscene racial slurs to one another, causing unnecessary violence in which, sometimes, lives are lost. I hope that this novel of a young boy can accurately portray the troubled times this country has faced, and what conflicts may occur, today. Fortunately, these kinds of hardships scarcely ever transpire, but no one will ever know what may smoke up in the future.

"I look confidently to the day when all who work for a living will be one with no thought to their separateness as Negroes, Jews, Italians or any other distinctions. This will be the day when we bring into full realization the American dream – a dream yet unfulfilled. A dream of equality of opportunity, of privilege and property widely distributed; a dream of a land where men will not take necessities from the many to give luxuries to the few; a dream of a land where men will not argue that the color of a man's skin determines the content of his character; a dream of a nation where all our gifts and resources are held not for ourselves alone, but as instruments of service for the rest of humanity; the dream of a country where every

man will respect the dignity and worth of the human personality." Martin Luther King, Jr.

Chapter 1

"*No one is born hating another person because of the color of his skin, or his background, or his religion. People must learn to hate, and if they can learn to hate, they can be taught to love, for love comes more naturally to the human heart than its opposite.*" Nelson Mandela

"... *for thine is the kingdom, the power, and the glory, forever, Amen.*" The few members of the Birmingham Presbyterian Church finished reciting the Lord's Prayer in unison and began to file out of the sanctuary. 12-year old Stuart Scott stood anxiously up from his seat and scurried through the pews until he finally approached an aged Reverend Paul, who stood waiting for the congregation to leave.

"Reverend, does Jesus love Rosa Parks? Does Jesus love those Negroes like Dr. King, Jr.? Does he love them people whose skin ain't like ours, Reverend?" Stuart asked blatantly, yearning for a response.

Reverend Paul gave an extended, uneasy stare at the young child, peering around the rather small altar to check if anyone had heard the uproar.

"My son, you remind me so much of your father when he was your age, asking so many intuitive questions. Jesus loves everybody, no matter what they look like. Now, I don't think this is a good time to talk about such an issue at this time…." Reverend Paul replied with an unresponsive tone, as he noticed Janice Scott, Stuart's mother waiting across the sanctuary. "Now, go on to your mother. She is waiting for you at the door."

Although he was dissatisfied with the reverend's response, Stuart graciously walked back to his mother and left the church.

"Stu darlin', is anything on your mind?" Mrs. Scott questioned her son, grabbing his arm tightly as they started to walk down the sidewalk.

"Nah mama, I'm fine. Let's go home; I don't wanna miss Ed Sullivan on television." Stuart sighed as it was obviously clear he had something on his mind. Several disturbing images he had seen on the news the week before began to pop up in his head rapidly. The week before, he had stayed up past his bed time; his mother was asleep and completely unaware of her son's actions. Stuart was watching the daily 10 o' clock news on television for a current events assignment at his school, when his attention was caught by images on the screen. The headline on the news had read in large letters, "NEGRO PROTESTS IN BIRMINGHAM, ALABAMA 1968 – A COMMOTION IN THE MAKING?" Several images of crowds of African-Americans rioting outside the local town hall had his mind swirling like a tornado.

Stuart Scott and his mother were not unfamiliar with living in the north side of Birmingham, Alabama, a white community. Stuart's father, Michael, was shot and killed while walking in the black-populated South side of town five years ago; late at night, he was abused for taking a shortcut home from work. Ever since the occurrence of the tragedy, Birmingham had transformed into a segregated community between the two sides, as most public facilities and events were reserved only for the whites, disregarding the black community. For years, the local streets had been inhabited by an army of protesters, who were perseverant in their fight for equality. In some cases, the crowds would evolve into dangerous free-for-all's, men and women of both races getting shoved and violently mixed around in a circle. It was no anomaly for Janice, as the owner of Scott's Pub, the most famous diner in town. She had witnessed almost everything from her building windows, calling the quarrels on the street, "the wrong kind of a melting pot." Unfortunately, she was no different from the other whites in Birmingham, as her diner was only allowed for people of the same color as she. Although Stuart was a seven-year-old boy back at the time of his father's tragic accident, he was still aware of the problems occurring in his town.

"Mama, where are we goin'? This isn't the way home…." Stuart glanced up at his mother and asked, glimpsing at her turquoise blue eyes that matched the cerulean blanket up above in the sky, slightly covered by the long, brunette curls dangling in front of her façade. Turning around a corner of the unknown street, the spring sun came out of its shelter, illuminating its rays upon Janice Scott's magenta dress in which Stuart held onto tightly with uncertainty. The strange neighborhood they had approached was as silent as a funeral; the "CLICK-CLICK" sound of Stuart's mother's high heels resonated throughout the area around them. From the ramshackle appearance of the several houses on that street, Stuart concluded that they had just walked down south, the section of town he hadn't encountered in over a year.

"Mama, why we walkin' down here?"

"It is the only place I can buy rice for supper darling. Now, just stay close to me, and don't you look at no nigger straight in the eye," Janice Scott replied, looking down at her scrawny son with a stern look on her face. She was reminded of all the saddening horrors that had followed her husband's death, and had made a promise to never let her son encounter any danger with an African-American. Stuart Scott was just an average, neighborhood southern White boy, attending an all-White boys' school that taught him the usual arithmetic and American vernacular. He was rather short for his age, around five feet but his deep, smoky, raspy voice had many of his friends question whether he had really sped through the stage of puberty at the speed of light. His butter blond hair hung down to his thin neck, with his sharp bangs veiling his minuscule, sapphire eyes, resembling his mother's. His crimson, red cheeks stood out in the brisk weather, corresponding to his tucked in, spotless, ruby polo shirt he was wearing that day. The slight, ruffled wind gusted along his checkered slacks that reached down to his shiny, charcoal black dress shoes. He was no admirer of this fancy attire on the Sabbath; Stuart felt most comfortable wearing his customary overalls that were hand-knitted precisely by his mother. At that moment, however, he felt the least comfortable walking in unknown territory.

"Mama … mama …. I don't wanna go here. I wanna go back home. I'm scared." Stuart whimpered impatiently, as they passed by an antiquated brick building that had a myriad of graffiti writings and signs on its walls. Still grasping onto his mother's arm, he glanced back to m ake out the words on the building, which said, "LIBRARY – BLACKS ONLY." He tried to scrutinize the different graffiti messages on the library walls, but his mother dragged him down the sidewalk. As both Stuart and his mother continued to trudge along the sidewalk, they heard slight noises of cars honking, bells chiming, and people chatting. With each step they took, the noises became more blatant, and more and more people, all African-Americans, were able to be distinguished.

"Honey, it will only take five minutes," Janice Scott whispered in Stuart's ear, as it was evidently difficult to communicate in the raucous city. To Stuart, the Southern part of Birmingham seemed like an absolutely different world compared to the North; most of the markets were located outside, the streets were occupied by many more citizens, and the public facilities were in poor condition. But most important of all, this "dirty hole," as the Northerners would say, was occupied by men and women of a different color, black. Stuart noticed the looks on several of the "negroes" faces as he walked into town; their eyes moved up and down on him and his mom, like a predator ready to pounce on its meal.

Stuart and his mother approached a rather immense, spacious building which appeared to be a market full of varieties of stands. Inside, it resembled a large garbage dump, as the floors were brimming with dirt stains and sticky residue. Since it was a Sunday afternoon, the markets were overloaded with customers; it was a challenge to even get near a food stand. Once the Scotts walked in, the commotion began to subside as the myriad of customers looked around at the unusual sight. Stuart's hands and body began to perspire in trepidation, as he clutched his mother's dress and arm even tighter than before. It was sheer silence for a few moments, until a gray-haired, plump African-American man appeared from the crowd, wearing a shirt that said, "Jimmy's Market."

"You fellas got no place in dis pat o' town. I reckon' ya both 'ken go back to yo' rich white hood an' don' botha' comin' back no mo," the old man yelled with vigor, gesturing them to walk out of the door. Stuart began to take a small step before his mother firmly stood her ground.

"I'm here to buy some grain, sir. I don't ask for no trouble, will you sell me some rice?" Janice graciously asked, opening up her small grocery sac in front of the man, whose name tag on his shirt read Morgan Freeman. He looked into her eyes for a second and rubbed his bushy beard to think, as the crowd of almost a hundred remained motionless.

"Lady an' yo chile' be praisin' the Lord, todeh. Hehehehe. All righ' y'all be thankin' the Lord fo' it's da Sabbath, but I be given ya no mo' den six poun's of dat rice."

"Sir, six pounds ain't enough for me to feed my family. Please, I walked all this time for a reward, and all I get is this?"

Suddenly, the crowd behind the old man Freeman started to mumble frantically as a sign of aversion to the reply. Stuart remained silent, but started to become more agitated with the situation at hand. The mumbles evolved into moderate conversations, which then turned into excessive shouts and taunts at Janice Scott.

"I warnin' you and yo' little boy. Ya take da six poun's o' grain, o you ain' gon' bak home, ma dear," Freeman shouted back, as the crowd of the African American customers began to move closer to Stuart and his mother, intimidating them. They began to spit heavily on Stuart and his mother's clothes, and threw minute fruit clippings from the ground towards their direction. In unison, the crowd yelled obnoxious chants of, "POWER TO THE NEGROES!"

Stuart looked up at his mother in shock and responded with tears, "Mama! Why are we standin' here? Let's go...."

"Finally, the relentless crowd of the market drove both Stuart and Janice out of the vicinity and into the streets; their clothes and dignity torn into pieces. Their faces were covered with foul spit, and their once elegant garments from Sunday Service earlier that day transformed into filthy rags.

"Mama ... why ... did you ... have to do that?" Stuart hesitantly asked, holding in tears as they began to walk back towards their neighborhood. "You know ... rice ain't important right now ... you almost go us killed, mama ...."

Through all the abuses that she and her son had just endured, the only thing that came out of her mouth was, "Now, you know what happened to Papa."

Chapter 2

"Every trial endured and weathered in the right spirit makes a soul nobler and stronger than it was before." James Buckham

"DDDRRRIIIINNNNGGGG," the deafening chime rung in Stuart's ear, as everyone in the classroom sprinted out, celebrating the end of the school day. For Stuart, the entire school day passed by in a flash, as all he could think about were the events that took place the night before. As Stuart walked out of the classroom door, he felt a rugged hand on his shoulder.

"Stu! Ready for another game of basketball? I've already got all the otherguys a the part right now, what's taking you so long? You all right? You ok? You don't seem right ... is something ..." his best friend Marc Anthony hurriedly rambled on, as Stuart was able to interrupt him.

"Yeah, I'm fine, I'll go meet you guys up at the park in a few. Just gotta go change."

Every day after school, Stuart and several of his best friends got together at the local Wheeler Park to play ball. They would call themselves "Birmingham's Best," a nickname given to them by Stuart's mother few years back because of their great friendship and trust. Stuart and his bests never hid anything from each other; they usually traveled to parties and games together, and they always had the same opinion on everything. But as Stuart walked lethargically onto the basketball court in the park, all of his buddies knew that something concerning was on his mind.

"Stu, you all right? You look like a kid who just lost his candy," his friend Rich Rowboat commented, bouncing a rubber basketball clamorously on the concrete. The rest of the crew stood in a circle, waiting for a response from their silent companion.

"I ... uh ... went down to the ... 'dirt hole' last night for the first time." Stuart finally answered, still staring down at the ground in shame.

When the other four of Stuart's friends heard what he had just said, they all had a puzzled look on their face. Rich Rowboat stopped dribbling the ball, and he seemed to be the only one asking Stuart how the situation turned out.

"Stu, please don't tell me you went to that part of town. It's where all those niggers live, those undeserving scums ... this is absolutely crazy, why didn't you tell us before you were going? We're not gonna let you wandering alone man ... I'm just scared somethin' would happen to you like what happened to your papa."

Finally, Stuart raised his head and looked at his fellow friends, who were anxiously waiting to hear his story. His forehead and cheeks turned a bright apple red as tears were flowing down his cheek. Wiping them away with his hand, he continued on.

"First of all, we're only 12 years old, and I ain't no fool about going anywhere alone. Anyways, Mama wanted for us to get some things for dinner at the market down there, and don't ask me why we decided to walk that far from the church."

"But there's a market right next door to the school ... and it was open all day, yesterday."

"I said, don't ask me why. Mama wanted her rice, so we walked down. Got it?"

As Stuart was recollecting his thoughts, the images of what had happened the night before began to reappear in cycles in his head. Finally, he released the uncontrollable anger inside of him.

"YOU KNOW WHAT? I'M SICK AND TIRED OF ALL THIS! YOU KNOW THEY DID TO ME? THEY SPIT ON ME. THEY THREW DIRT ON ME. THOSE NIGGERS PUSHED ME. YOU GUYS DON'T KNOW WHAT MY PAPA WENT THROUGH. AND DON'T EVER TRY TO GET IN THE M IDDLE OF IT...."

Unable to control his feelings, Stuart broke down to the ground and wept. The rest of his friends tried to console him as they all kneeled down with him. Speechless by what had occurred to his friend, Marc Anthony whispered in Stuart's ear:

"Stu, one day we're gonna kick those bastards out of this town. Negroes don't belong in Birmingham. Hell, they don't belong in America."

Finally, with one last thought in his head, Stuart said:

"I just pray to God that this will all end...."

Not only did Stuart have his share of troubles during his week at school; at Scott's Pub, it seemed as everything was at its usual, quick pace, except for Janice Scott. To support Stuart and herself, she, as the owner of the famous diner, had to sometimes work ten hours, six days a week. This time of the year during spring, customers were in and out like a speed train, and all of the employees at the pub had no reason to lack concentration. Unfortunately for Janice, she struggled trying to pull herself together, and take multiple food orders at one time. On that horrific Sunday night, she had suffered minor cuts and bruises on her face from the rampage at the market. She tried her best to cover up all the scars on her skin, and act like nothing had occurred. But just as her own son experienced an emotional breakdown at the park, she couldn't continue delivering dishes, as one day, one of her female employees, Sheila, brought her into the kitchen bathroom to privately console her.

"Janice, what's that on your face?" Sheila asked worriedly, as she laid her fingers on Janice's silky, powdered face, slowly feeling the bumps that were concealed under the make-up. "Oh, my goodness, what happened to you?"

The two women were both sitting down uncomfortably on the floor, as the crashing sounds of dishes thrown into sinks could be heard through the bathroom door. A tear ran down Janice's glimmering cheek, revealing a small trace of a scrape on her face.

"I needed to get rice for the kitchen ... so I went down to a market down south, and they threatened me and my baby. This is what happened," Janice replied, pointing to the different scars on her body. For Janice, the biggest scar on her was on the inside; whenever she would be reminded of the despicable actions of the African-American community, it'd feel like a bullet going through her heart.

"Oh, Jesus, why didn't you report this to the police? Stay here, let me call them, and I'll go get a doctor for you to check ...." Sheila hesitantly replied, as she got up to try to find the nearest telephone. She opened the bathroom door quickly, and at the sight of the hectic commotion of the kitchen, Janice grabbed Sheila by the arm and stopped her.

"No, I'll just go after work, hun. We've got too many customers on our hands, and I don't want this to slow us down. Just please don't tell anyone .... Thanks."

For a moment, Sheila looked into her manager's eyes with concern, and then hastily trudged out of the kitchen to take care of the many anxious and furious waiting customers at the door. Janice inhaled a deep breath and calmly closed her eyes, clashes of her husband emerging in her mind.

"Oh, Michael, this wasn't the way I wanted it to be. I miss you so …."

Suddenly, as she was whispering to herself, Sheila jogged back to the kitchen, gasping for air like she had just run a marathon.

"Janice, your son is here. He wants to see you."

"Oh, sorry … uh … wait, why is Stuart, here?" Janice questioned her employee as if she was waiting for a response back. Then, she gazed around the still raucous atmosphere until she finally recognized a clock, reading "4:00." Janice fixed her stained diner gown, and walked out into the dining area, noticing each and every table occupied. A myriad of tumultuous noises intermingled in the air. The perpetual clanging of silverware, the rambunctious exchange between the usual senior citizens of town, and the booming chorus of Bob Dylan's *"Like A Rolling Stone"* rung in Janice's eardrums, as she forced her way through the constricted aisles of the restaurant towards Stuart, who stood adjacent to the entrance and exit doors. Wearing a dark, shabby t-shirt, smudged soccer shorts, and threadbare sneakers, Stuart still carried his school backpack, as his mother was able to perceive that he had just come back from the park.

"Baby, what are you doing here? I told you before that you should never come here after school. Now, go home darliin'; I can't talk to you, now." Janice shouted in her son's ear, making sure he would be able to comprehend throughout all the pandemonium that was going on around them.

"Mama, I'm too scared to walk alone anywhere, now. I wanna go home with you. I'll wait; I'll do anything to help around." Stuart distressingly responded.

"Honey, I told you already that you cannot stay here! You'll be okay; it only takes less than ten minutes to get home. Now, go on...."

"You don't know what's goin' on out there, mama. There's a riot few blocks away, and those black people are comin' this way. I don't wanna roam around in those streets and get into more trouble."

For a moment, Janice stood in silence in front of her son, and with no hesitation, she whispered in his ear, "You're in charge of the counter for the rest of the day."

Chapter 3

"It is to the credit of human nature, that except where its selfishness is brought into play, it loves more readily than it hates. Hatred, by a gradual and quiet process, will even be transformed to love, unless the change be impeded by a continually new irritation of the original feeling of hostility."
Nathaniel Hawthorne

Stuart entered the cashier's booth of the diner, clueless like a deer before headlights. Having no experience at work, or even touching a dollar bill, he was thinking, "Now, what in the world have I gotten myself into?" Fortunately for Stuart, as the minutes went by and by, customers were beginning to file out of the restaurant at the sight of the setting sun. The employees at the dinner were apparently bitter about the peculiar situation of the daytime abeyance starting at such an early time. The noise level drastically dropped, and there were only a few customers still finishing up their supper.

"All right, it's almost five. I think I'll be alright by myself with Stu, so you guys can make your way home, now. I'll close the place on my own, tonight." Janice announced to her several employees who were drenched in sweat from the vigorous work. They took off their grimy work uniforms and threw them into the kitchen sink, ready for a wash for the next day.

"Good night, have a safe trip home." Stuart kindly said to the last remaining customers as they walked out the doors next to him. He looked at the clock on the wall behind him, which read, "5:00." His mother and the rest of the employees were in the back kitchen, leaving just him alone in the dining area. "This is weird, I though the riot was coming towards this way...," he thought to himself as he scrutinized out the windows. All he could perceive through the dark, foggy glass was the local post office across the street, and only a few people walking on the sidewalk. Finally, his mother appeared from the kitchen doors holding two brooms and some wet rags. The pungent, raunchy aroma of the kitchen accosted Stuart's nostrils, as he turned the radio off from under the cashier table, waiting for his mother's request.

"Thanks for helping out baby, we did need you today. It was pretty hectic in here ... well, can you just grab these and just clean the tables and the floor. The rest just left through the back, and I'll go lock the doors."

"Alright ... Mama, I'm sorry for saying I wanted to go home before. I really thought those guys were coming back to cause trouble around town. I was wrong."

"Oh baby, it's ok. We'll walk home together; there's nothing to be worried about. It's nice and quiet out, and you don't be scared. Boy, you look like you're starvin'. Have some of this." Janice smiled, handed her son a small piece of bread, and gave a small kiss on her son's cheek.

Stuart was able to eye-ball the numerous scratches on his mother's delicate skin and felt the rough scrapes with his fingers. He decided to remain silent and started to go around the tables. As the day grew weary, both Janice and Stuart were beginning to leave the events from the night before, in the back of their minds. They just wanted to get rid of the miserable pain that had clouded their heads the entire day. Minutes passed by as both of them continued to scrub the different areas of the restaurant until suddenly, unusual, reiterating noises, like the pounding of drums, began to ring in their ears. For a moment, Stuart dropped his broom on the ground, curious to see where the uproar was coming from.

"Mama, you heard that?" he looked back at Janice and asked, puzzled.

"I think it's coming from outside. Stu, go look out the windows and see what it is. Don't tell me it's another protest...." Janice replied sounding a bit dismayed knowing that her walk home would be another gruesome task. For almost 10 years since she first opened up her joint, random protests from the Black community would storm onto the streets in front of the diner, forcing Janice to avoid the perturbation and walk a different, much longer route home.

"Yup, mama, they're finally here. I see them carrying those signs like they did on TV, and all that ... what are they doing?" Stuart inquired, standing up on front of the entrance doors, looking eagerly at the situation outside. He couldn't count the massive line of African-Americans, young and old, who were commanding the streets towards the town hall like an army, determined to fight whatever would come their way. The shouts were becoming increasingly boisterous, booming enough to be heard inside the diner.

"Mama, can I go outside to see what's going on?"

"You must be playing dear! In no way you will encounter such danger again like this! Now, just stay in, and we'll just wait until this is over."

"But mama, for only just a bit. It's gonna be forever until we get back home."

"NO!"

Disgruntled with the response, Stuart remained to look out the windows; the outside was gradually becoming darker and the protests were transforming into a wild rampage. Unexpectedly, troops of police cars were beginning to appear in great numbers, as the African-Americans on the streets started to flee from the scene.

"MAMA, LOOK!   THE POLICE ARE HERE."   Stuart exclaimed, as a stampede of fretful Blacks attempted to escape the madness.

His eyes were glued to the policemen who rapidly jumped out of their cars, driving away the herd of people. Although it seemed as Stuart's view was too distant, he was able to witness pepper spray in the air, allowing some of the about 20 policemen to track down the hopefuls. This was the first time he was ever witnessing this kind of frenzy in real life, for he would only watch or read of these rallies either on television or in the daily paper. Stuart never imagined at a young age, that he would see desperate people jumping over others, stumbling and suffering injuries on the ground, and howling from the foul effects of pepper spray; it seemed way too surreal for him.

"Alright now, I think it's time for you to stop watching all of this, baby, and just sit down for a bit. I'm gonna turn off the lights, and we're gonna go through the back door." Janice said over her son's shoulder, making sure he wasn't too engaged in the wildness.

Finally as Stuart began to turn away, he was startled at the sight of someone in front of the diner door. For a second his heart sunk in trepidation as the strange fellow, lying on his side on the front steps of the dinner, was clearly in pain. Stuart sharply looked around him, noticing his mother walked to the back of the kitchen. Then, he turned back around and realized the person, who appeared to be a young African-American boy, was clenching his legs, blood dripping down to his feet. Stuart watched in awe from the window, as he just stood there motionless. The policemen continued to push the crowd farther back and back, and the little boy began to bang on the locked door of the diner, urging for Stuart to help.

"Stuart, stop banging on the door for Christ's sake! Now, hurry up so we can go home!" Janice yelled from the back kitchen, as she was unaware that her son was not the one pounding on the glass. Stuart stood up quickly, as he could feel the impulses in his body rapidly moving.

"Oh my goodness, should I help him out? Should I just leave him? Mama will hate me forever if I bring him inside...." Stuart pondered as his mind was vacillating between the two sides like a pendulum. The little boy on the ground continued to pound on the door, sobbing in torment as he was desperately crying for help. Inside, Stuart felt torn, as flashbacks of that Sunday night were again protruding his brain.

He knew that those African-Americans treated him like a doormat, and he began to question himself, "Why should I feel sorry for this suffering boy? His people gave us nothing but dirt to us, so why should we be able to help him? I should just walk back to mama and go home."

But instead, he couldn't bear the misery, for he glanced one more time into the hurting stranger's eyes; each teardrop that fell down his scraped cheek felt like a stab to Stuart's heart. He had never seen anyone agonize in such anguish as this African-American boy.

"Stuart, what is going on there? I'm coming for you right now," Janice proclaimed as Stuart was able to hear the irritability in his mother's voice. He didn't care to respond, as he sprinted to the cashier's booth to grab the door key from inside a drawer. Stuart decided to put all of the aversion and frustration from the brutal night in the past, for he felt obligated to possibly save this stranger's life. His entire body continued to tremble as he slipped the key through the lock on the door.

Finally, at the click of the lock, Stuart pushed open the glass entrance door and gingerly carried the miniscule boy onto the diner floor. Stuart relocked the door shut, as he looked down at the squirming boy, who was breathing heavily like he was unconscious. Stuart, afraid his mother would discover the stranger in their diner, attempted to carry his fragile body behind the cashier booth. But as he began to lift him up, he heard a voice from behind, "Stu...art ... wha...."

Janice couldn't continue her words, as she fainted to the ground.

Chapter 4

"Friendship needs no words – it is solitude, delivered from the anguish of loneliness," Dag Hammarskjold

"So Doctor, will my mama be all right?" Stuart asked with an impatient look on his face. He sat next to his mother on the ground, as she was lying down and being treated by the local physician.

"Your mother will be just fine. She just experienced a little unconsciousness, but luckily you, little boy, were able to call me just in time. I was almost done with my shift, until this happened. She's going to be fine, but she just needs some rest. And, uh … who is this black boy standing here? I thought there ain't supposed to be no Negroes in here, Stu," the doctor replied, as he pointed to the other African-American boy who was sitting on one of the dinner tables, grabbing his bloody leg.

"I don't know, doctor. There was something goin' on outside with the cops an hour ago, and this guy was bangin' on my door as I was gonna leave for home. Then, I noticed he was cryin', and shakin', and I felt bad so I let him in. I tried talking to him, and he hasn't said anything, sir. I just gave him a few wet towels to wash his knee. That's all."

The doctor stood up from the ground and looked straight into the strange little boy's hazel eyes as if he had never seen an African-American person ever before in his life.

"Boy, what's your name?" the doctor asked in a demanding tone.

The little boy appeared to be startled at the question, as he crept back in his seat. He remained silent and continued to press down on his impaired leg, hoping that no one would harm him in any way. The boy had rather short and very curly, black hair that hung over his smoky, colored eyes. His infant-like round face and pointed ears resembled the man's façade Stuart encountered at the market that past Sunday. The little stranger wore a threadbare, white t-shirt that had once been tight, but stretched out tremendously from the riot. His lanky legs were plastered in dust from the rocks outside, bordering the ripped holes in his shorts. Blood continued to drip from his ankles down to the leather on his shabby sandals, as some of the scarlet fluid dried up on his toes.

"Boy, answer me!" the doctor ordered, as the tone of his voice was becoming huskier with anger. Still, there was no response from the quiet stranger; Stuart walked over to the doctor, hoping to ease his frustration.

"Sir, don't yell at him. You're just gonna make it worse...," Stuart cautiously said, as he remained next to his sleeping mother.

"Nigger, why aren't you answering me?" yelled the doctor as he finally unleashed his fury by slapping the little boy's face, as loud as a crack of thunder. This shocked Stuart, as he saw a bright, blushing bruise on the stranger's face, the size of a prune. Tears reappeared from the little boy's eyes, rolling down his rutted face. Then, the doctor looked down at the body's injured leg and smirked. He didn't even bother treating the stranger's wound, as he walked back out of the restaurant in rage. As he was on his way out of the door, Stuart was able to make out some words mumbled under the doctor's mouth, "I don't help no niggers. All just poor pieces of trash around here." Both Stuart and the African-American boy, who appeared to be about the same age as he, were extremely confused by the doctor's temperament, as Stuart got up and walked over to the nameless stranger.

"Hey ... uh ... boy, tell me your name. I won't hurt you. I just wanna help."

Stuart was beginning to feel as if this strange African-American boy, who had just been caught up in a middle of a riot outside, had some sort of disease or disorder that impaired his speech. For the past few hours they were secluded inside the diner, Stuart had not seen the boy's mouth budge once.

"You know what, I'm sick of this. You won't talk to me. I'm trying to do my best to help; this is useless. It's getting late. You better go home, now. NOW!" Stuart stood up with vengeance from the diner seat and marched toward his sleeping mother. As he was bending over to wake his mother up, he heard a faint whisper from behind and quickly turned around.

"What did you just say?"

"M...my ...I ...uh ...." The little boy's lips were beginning to churn, as the words coming from his mouth were indistinguishable. Stuart walked over closer to the African-American boy, and he stuck out his ears, eager for a distinct response. "I ... ma ... freema...freeman ...."

"I'm a freeman? What?" Stuart was very perplexed by what the little boy was urging. "I ... ma ... Freeman. Tha...that ... is ... ma ... n...name...," the younger teenager replied, hoping that Stuart would comprehend his struggle to pull out words from inside.

"Your name ... Ima Freeman?"

"Ima Freeman. Dat's ... ma name," the boy Ima whimpered, still a bit petrified from his unknown surroundings. Ima limped up from his seat and stood up, still leaning forward a little bit from the sting on his leg. The bleeding stopped, and now Stuart stood face to face with the boy who he had just "rescued" from the wild commotion hours before. Inside his head Stuart was thinking, "I must be dreaming right now. It's past bedtime, gotta go to school tomorrow, but now I'm stuck in the diner with a stranger standin' across from me." Stuart was beginning to feel dizzy from the extreme sequence of events, and didn't know what he was going to do next."

"Ima, that's your name?"

"Yis."

"Where you come from?"

"Otis Park."

Stuart was ready to challenge Ima with another question, but the words, "Otis Park" stood out in his mind. He began to think acutely, trying to remember where he had seen those words before. Images of different parts of Birmingham began to swirl in Stuart's mind like a tornado, trying to grasp where that park was located. Finally, he was reminded of that dreadful Sunday night at the south side of town. Walking down the sidewalk with his mother, he had seen those words, "Otis Park" on a small billboard outside a garage building. Suddenly, he recognized that those exact words were also imprinted on the shirt of that man who had mocked both Stuart and his mother at Jimmy's Market.

"Wait, your last name is Freeman?"

"Uh ... yeah ... why?"

Stuart felt his heart sink rapidly like a submarine, as he recalled that man at the market: Morgan Freeman. In his head, he knew that these two people were related to one another, but he decided not to reveal it to Ima, for he did not want to spark any more turmoil.

"It's just … never mind … why did you come here?"

"Ma popa tol' me to pick up rolls and a' juice fo' dinna. I gotta caught en da pack of dem peeps who was hootin' and hollerin' ou'side."

Stuart was in awe, as he realized that Ima was put in the same situation as Stuart and his mother had been earlier that week. "Is this some coincidence? I must really be dreaming…" Stuart thought, smacking his head to figure out whether he was in a daze.

"Ya know? My pops don' like no whit' color fellas like you. Yous jus' a nice boy fo' savin' me. Thank ya'."

Stuart wasn't fond of the tone and accent of Ima's walking, as it was virtually impossible to grasp what the strange boy was trying to say. But he was able to hear Ima's appreciation for him, which dug deep into his heart. Stuart peered past the standing Ima at the immense sign that hung in front of the diner's entrance. "WHITES ONLY," the bold, black letters showed as Stuart's mind was racing once more. He looked behind at his resting mother, knowing that if she had waken up at the sight of an African-American boy in her restaurant, she would punish Stuart to a pulp.

Stuart and Ima began to engage in a normal conversation; seconds turned into minutes, and minutes were finally turning into hours. Outside, it was pitch black like an abyss; there were no people on the streets, as the clock struck midnight. The bright, fluorescent lights of the diner continued to shine, and the two boys continued to talk, unaware of the time. Stuart continued to provide Ima with help on his leg, and realized that he and his mother would remain in the restaurant for the night.

"Ima, you know how to read?"

"Eh, a bit. I no' da alphabet, dat's all I need ta know, right?"

"Well then, go to the front of the door, and read what the sign says."

Stuart dragged Ima's gangly arms towards the entrance and pointed at the ponderous sign.

"Uh ... whi...white...whites! Dat right?"

Stuart nodded in agreement.

"On...onl...only? Whites Only?"

Ima was able to decipher the ominous message on the front of the diner, incredibly surprising Stuart. Ima cracked a tiny smile, as Stuart looked at his unusual African-American boy. All of his assumptions of "Negroes" not being able to read were finally slaughtered. After his father's death, Stuart had never expected to meet a "black" person ever in his life. Until that moment, Janice had taught him to avoid all men, women, and children of colored skin, telling Stuart that they were just "doormats." Of course, Stuart was only a growing adolescent at the age of 12. He figured, "Let me just experience for myself; I don't need mama tellin' me who to like or who to hate." Stuart was the most intellectual person in his clan, "Birmingham's Best," and his other friends would remind him to stay aloof from the African-American community. For years, Stuart had been corrupted by his own peers, and for the first time, he was able to look through the eyes of a struggling African-American boy. Inside, he identified the consequences he would face if the white community found out about the developing friendship between himself and Ima. He was afraid of the backlash he would eventually receive, for this bond would create harsher tension between the north side and south side of Birmingham.

"Ima, it's almost midnight. I think it's time you go home, now. I won't tell mama that you stayed here for this long."

"Buh...yo Stu?"

"Yeah?"

"Ma poppa gon' killa me when I go back...."

Just when Ima replied in a very apprehensive voice, Stuart gave a word of advice to his new acquaintance.

"Ima, you listen to me. Your poppa isn't gonna know anything about what happened, today. You have to promise me, now; we keep all of this just between me and you, and no one else. You probably know this, Ima, but we're in a war, right now. It's bad. Really bad. We're tryin' to get rid of you guys, and you guys are tryin' to get rid of us. Simple as that. I'm tellin' you this because we're smaller than anybody in this town. But together, we can change that. I'm not sayin' that you try to tell your people that we should all come together real quickly. It's not gonna work that way. It's gonna take time, Ima. I know it. I watch the late news every night, and I sneak into my livin' room because momma tells me the news don't tell me anything. They're tryin' to make us all mad and go fight each other in the streets. People are sufferin', just like you did before. Look at your leg, Ima; see that cut? That's nothin' compared to what happened to the others who tried to stop all this. Dr. King took a bullet for what he tried to do! The townspeople here are too stupid, and they just judgin' you by the color on your skin. So I'm tellin' you, Ima, you go home tonight, and you have a nice sleep. You wake up tomorrow mornin', forget about what anyone tells you, and don't be afraid of no one. We can change all of this together, Ima. Trust me."

Ima looked down at his scraped knee once more and firmly nodded to Stuart's appreciation. From the expression on his stern face, Ima was clearly aware of the situation surrounding not only his family and his community, but also the entire country. Then, he pulled his hand out from his pocket towards Stuart. The two shook hands and grinned with hope.

"Stu, I be o' my way home, but whe' do we see each otha' agin?"

"Tomorrow, behind the diner in the alleyway next to the kitchen. 4:00. Don't tell no one."

"See ya, Stu!"

Ima tiptoed towards the entrance of the restaurant, hoping he wouldn't create any noise to wake Janice up from the ground. Finally, Stuart delicately unlocked the doors, as Ima cautiously trudged out.

"Ima! Remember!" Stuart panted, as his new friend ran away in the darkness.

Chapter 5

"The glory of friendship is not the outstretched hand, nor the kindly smile nor the joy of companionship; it is the spiritual inspiration that comes to one when he discovers that someone else believes in him and is willing to trust him." Ralph Waldo Emerson

"Mama ... MAMA!" Stuart nudged his mother, who still remained asleep on the diner ground. The glimmering sun began to wake up from its sleep as its rays shone brightly through the windows of the restaurant. Stuart had been woken up by the piercing sound of the grandfather's clock on the counter wall, as it showed five past six. He was sluggish to get up from his sleep and noticed the diner was opening in less than a half hour. "Mama, wake up! I gotta get to school now...."

Finally, Janice opened her weary eyes and looked at Stuart like he was some kind of stranger. Then, she jumped right up to her feet in surprise and started panicking.

"Wh...what happened? I .... don't remember sleepin' here.... Baby, what time is it? How did I end up here?"

"Mama, it's fine, stop worryin'. It's almost time to open and none of your workers ain't here, yet."

"Alright now, you go off to school. I'll be fine for the first few hours, won't be expectin' many folks comin' in this morning. Stuart, what happened last night .... I seemed to have forgotten everythin'...."

When Janice said her last few words, Stuart was about to blurb out every little detail that occurred between him and Ima. Instead, he hesitated and was reminded of a certain incident, the moment he saw his mother fall to the ground at the sight of an African-American boy walk in to her store. Stuart knew his mother was not aware of the new friendship he had made with an "enemy," according to Janice, and he was sure to keep the bond a secret. He knew that if his mother found out about Ima, Stuart would be punished severely.

"Oh, uh ... nothin' mama. It was just rowdy outside last night, and I didn't want us to walk home so late. I reckon it was a good idea to sleep here for the night." Stuart lied to his mother, as he grabbed his backpack from behind the diner counter. "Anyway, I've gotta get to school, now, mama. I'll see ya."

Stuart leaned over to his plump-faced mother, who was leaning on one of the restaurant tables and gave her a peck on the cheek. Stuart, wearing the same ragged clothes from the day before, walked out the diner doors and into a new, fresh, spring morning. His school, P.S. 112, the only white junior high school in Birmingham, was located just three blocks away from Scott's Pub, which made his trek a much easier one. He was able to hear the myriad of cars dropping off students one by one, and the shrill movements of the kids before class. Usually every morning, Stuart and his best friends, Marc Anthony and Rich Rowboat, would either walk or bike the three miles to school together. However, on this morning, Marc and Rich were waiting outside the busy school's doors, waiting for their absent friend to appear. At the sound of the bell, which signaled the beginning of school, a stampede of students

Korean-American Voices of Youth in New Jersey

rammed through to their classes like cheetah, pushing kids right an left of them. Finally, as the commotion settled down, Marc and Rich were the only two students left, as they anxiously waited outside the school. Five minutes later, they noticed a running Stuart carrying a backpack from a distance.

"Stu ... where the hell have you been?" Marc asked impatiently.

"Sorry, I wasn't home this morning and I couldn't let you guys know," Stuart replied breathing heavily.

"Well, we can OBVIOUSLY see that...." Rich glared at Stuart with a distressed look, as if Stuart had befriended him.

"You guys didn't have to wait for me, hurry we're late for...."

Stuart was interrupted abruptly by Marc, whose folded arms and tapping feet made Stuart a bit uneasy.

"You know Stu ... you've been actin' real strange lately. Richie and I have been tryin' to call you, but you ain't picked up once. Not once ... and yesterday at the park? You were just hollerin' like something poked you on the butt. Whatever's goin' on, tell us now."

Stuart felt his heart swing like a pendulum. "I don't know what I did wrong to make them mad...," he thought, trying to find a solution to his friend's request.

"I ... uh ... Marc, I ...."

"You know what? Rich, let's just go to class. Let's leave him alone. We're just wastin' our time and we're late." Marc cut off Stuart, who was eager to find words to say. Marc and Rich grabbed their backpacks from the steps of the school, turned around, and walked in, leaving Stuart alone by himself sitting on a wooden bench outside the doors. Inside, he felt as if the world was collapsing; he lowered his head down to his knees and started to cry.

"God … why did you have to make people hate? I didn't do nothin' … no one understands me…," Stuart pouted under his own arms, wiping away the tears of sadness. He felt listless, and for the next few hours, he lied on the school bench outside unnoticed and slept. He couldn't walk through those school doors, his appearance making him resemble a beggar. All he could dream of was to go back in time and relive his past three days over again. Stuart would've never been spit on after church, he would've never gotten into an argument with his best friends, nor he would've slept at the diner for the first time in his life. Stuart was feeling regret, shame, and melancholy at the same time, as he was searching for an answer to all of his troubles.

"DING! DING!" The school's afternoon bell was set off noisily, as Stuart stormed up from his deep sleep. He put on his backpack and stood up, thinking of where he should go next. The diner was not an option, for his mother would become furious at her son's skipping of school. Then, he realized sharply the promise he had made to Ima the night before.

"Tomorrow, behind the diner in the alleyway next to the kitchen. 4:00. Don't tell no one."

Stuart slowly took off from the school's vicinity, walking back towards the restaurant. It took a couple of minutes before he finally reached the very secluded, shady alleyway behind Scott's Pub. Without notice by his mother, Stuart snuck through two building walls and found himself sitting on the grimy concrete, filled with scrapings of food. There was a strong, pungent, and unpleasant aroma that came from the garbage tanks adjacent to the sitting Stuart, as he covered his face from the horrid smell. He figured that this "junk hole," according to Janice, would be the only spot where he and Ima could not be found. Stuart stared at his watch, which read "2:00," as he realized he had two hours to spare. A couple feet away from his feet, Stuart found a rusted newspaper that was lying halfway in a tiny mud puddle. The filthy cover read, "Jefferson County Tribune – May 15, 1968," that showed a blurry image of several African-Americans holding up signs on a street. Under the picture, there was a caption that Stuart read aloud, "Night of May 14; several Negroes protesting outsider Rucker Ave. after law is passed, banning bus transportation for African-Americans in Birmingham, Alabama."

Stuart was intrigued by the headline, as he concluded that the image was taken from the night before. He continued to read on through the mucky article, fascinated by the ongoing feud that was printed in the newspaper. From article to article, Stuart couldn't impede his eyes from reading countless stories about new laws passed, and viewing photos and other images of policemen arresting groups of African-Americans. Finally after an hour of reading, Stuart finished the newspaper and stuck the grubby issue in his backpack, hoping to hide it from his mother. He stood up lethargically and stretched, looking around to see if Ima had appeared, yet. Exhausted from the foul odor in the alley, Stuart decided to trudge out of the crammed area, but before he was able to walk out in the open, he was startled by a bizarre, shrill noise coming from behind.

"Who is that?" Stuart turned around in a swift motion, as there was nobody to be seen. Feeling apprehensive and suspicious, he decided to move back to where he sat before and slowly walked towards where the strange sound had come from. In protection, he swung his backpack around from his back and used it as a shield in front of himself. Suddenly as he was inching closer and closer to the garbage dump, he heard another noise but his time, Stuart was able to conclude that it was a hushed, raspy voice of a person.

"Stu ... Stu ... is dat you?"

"Who is ... Ima? Is that you behind the dump?"

"Yeah, hel' me over dis crate."

Stuart stepped on a milk crate to see over the lofty garbage dump and noticed Ima, who was wearing much nicer attire than the night before. There was a railing in between Ima and the garbage dump, and as Ima attempted to climb the fence, Stuart grabbed his slender arms and pulled him over to his side.

"Boy, ya' betta' know whe' da right' time t' come is ... almos' got me kill'."

"What? Did something happen? Do your parents know?"

"Na' Stu, jus' walkin' down here en couple o' yo' white folks runnin' afta me? I call it nuts. Dey yellin, 'Run away, we don' want no niggas in dis place ..... I she' nuttin' man."

Stuart, a little disturbed by Ima's response, opened up his backpack and pulled out the newspaper he had read and found before, hoping to change the subject.

"Check this out. Ima, read it." Stuart handed the paper over to Ima, who stared at the paper with a look of perplexity on his face. Ima turned the smudged newspaper in circles as if he had no idea what to do with it.

"I dun' know how t' rea'." Ima handed the newspaper back to Stuart.

"Well, it just says you guys can't use the bus here no more."

"Who 'you guys' mean?" Ima asked, shrugging his shoulders as Stuart rolled his eyes in laughter.

"Who else can 'you guys' mean, Ima? Colored peeps. Like you." Stuart responded playfully, as Ima finally understood the meaning. "Now, THIS is what the problem is, Ima. You guys ain't treated the way we are. Just look at you. You were chased on your way, here. It's crazy out there. I wanna find a way to change this."

"The' why dun I tell ma folks back hom 'bout dis?"

"If you tell either your mama or papa, they gonna tell their people 'bout what we doin' and they're just gonna start more fighting. You know what? I just want all of this hate to be over. That's my dream. One day, I wish we could just live with no people dyin' on the streets, and nobody chasin' after one another and killin' people." Stuart responded loudly, as sounds of silverware coming from inside the diner were audible. Then, both Stuart and Ima looked at one another as voices of the employees were able to be heard, saying, "I think someone's out there...." In danger of being found in the alleyway, the two friends sprinted out of the area and into the streets.

"WHERE ARE WE GOIN'?!?" Ima yelled as the beeping of cars and the other noisy sounds of town overpowered his shouting. They continued to run away from the restaurant together, people on the sidewalk staring at the strange duo.

"JUST FOLLOW ME!" Stuart screamed with a heavy breath. For minutes straight, the two boys continued to run through the busy crowds of downtown Birmingham, dodging the townspeople one by one like a race. Soon enough, they became fatigued and stopped in a much quieter neighborhood.

"This is my neighborhood ... it seems like school isn't over, yet. Don't see any kids around...," Stuart uttered, breathing heavily from the excess running. "Ima, you don't go to school?"

Ima, exhausted from the continuous sprint, needed some time before he could respond.

"Uh ... nah ... I she' it's a bes' fo' me to go back home now ... dis ain't a goo' idea, Stu."

"What? Just come to my house for a bit, I'll get you some lemonade. We have to figure somethin' out. Let's go." Before Ima was able to respond, Stuart pulled him by the shirt like a toy and led him towards his house. The streets were empty, and the only sound heard came from the bright chirps of the flock of birds in the air. They finally reached the front of the Scott's lawn which seemed like an entire new place for Stuart, considering he had not stepped foot in his own home for a while. As the two walked up the steps and onto the porch, they were startled by familiar voices from behind.

"Stu, decide to skip school, today, buddy?"

Both boys looked around swiftly, and Stuart noticed it was Rich and Mark standing several feet away from them. They were holding their backpacks, as several little school children walked behind with their parents. Stuart realized that school had finished, and when his two friends called out his name, he began to feel uneasy.

"Uh … yeah … I felt kinda …." Before he could continue, he was interrupted by Marc, again.

"AND, who is that next to you? HEY, WHO THE HELL ARE YOU, BOY?!?" he said in an irritated voice, as both he and Rich began to walk closer towards the other two frozen boys. Ima tried conceal his face by putting his head down, and peeked behind the taller Stuart. Still, there was no response from the two, as Rich pushed Stuart away to reveal the scared Ima.

"Wait, isn't this the kid we saw runnin' downtown just an hour ago, Marc?"

Marc nodded and lifted the sweaty chin of Ima, trying to get a better look on him.

"Yeah, what the hell is he doing here? Stu, who is this?" Marc replied.

The fuming Stuart knocked Marc's hand off of Ima's face and stood in front of the silent boy.

"Now, what does it matter to you who it is? I thought you guys were too busy in 'school', and you guys tryin' to accuse me of having a friend over?"

Rich and Marc stared at one another and began chuckling at their changed friend. Before they turned around and decided to part ways, Rich had one more thing to say, "You know, Stu? I thought we could always trust you as a friend. I thought we would share all of our problems together and not worry about nothin'. Now, you're actin' like some stranger, like some kind of ... enemy. You not comin' to school with us together, not tellin' us about some cheap black friend you've got there ... you know? For all this time, I thought you were a good friend to me. Now, you just wanna ditch us for some dirt? I can't believe it ... you will pay for this, Stu. Better watch your back, next time." Finally, the two boys went off in the distance, leaving Stuart and the hidden Ima alone.

"I'mma sorry man, I dun' want dis to be dis weh." Ima tearfully cried, as Stuart comforted his saddened friend by walking him back inside the house.

"Don't worry about it, Ima. They don't understand. They just don't understand...."

They walked into the spacious home, illuminated by the radiant rays of the sun peeking through the windows. The smell of fresh, firewood logs from the fireplace accosted the two boys' nostrils, as Ima was fascinated by the mundane furniture and paintings inside the home.

"I neva see anytin' like dis," he said in amazement, as he walked around the wooded living room, staring at the Scott family portraits hanging up on the wall. Stuart walked into his kitchen and grabbed two cans of lemonade from his refrigerator.

Then, he turned on his antiquated radio next to the sofa; the smooth voice of Roy Orbison's *"Pretty Woman"* reverberating the room.

"Dis ya' mama and papa?" Ima pointed at one of the many portraits on the wall, holding and sipping an ice cold lemonade in his other hand.

"Yeah, that's it. I'm the only child." Stuart said, standing adjacent to his eager friend.

"I see yo' mama befo' … weh yo' papa?"

"My papa died few years back … was shot and killed …. Still remember that day, today…." Stuart replied in a subtle tone, trying not to recall those tragic moments.

"I'mma so sorry brotha' … you find ou' who dun' it?"

"Mama tells me just some blacks found my papa comin' home from work. She tells me they beat him and shoot him, but I think she ain't tellin' me the truth. I just say Jesus took him to a better place … you believe in him?"

"Papa tellin' me dat church jus' a wase a time. I she' nuttin' 'bout Jesus, God, the Bible, dun' know nuttin'."

Stuart stared at Ima, who shrugged his shoulders and continued to look at the photos on the wall. Then, he looked at his father in one of the portraits, thinking of how his father would always tell him stories from the Bible and all of the times his father would bring him to Sunday Service, every week. He remembered the day of his seventh birthday; Stuart had received a gold necklace of a cross from his father. When he was given this necklace, Stuart was told the exact words from his father. "Whenever you feel lonely or afraid, close your eyes, hold onto this necklace, and god will protect you from anything."

That moment was the first time in Stuart's life that he felt invincible, but just months after receiving the gold chain, his father's tragic death would leave him questioning his own faith.

Ever since the passing, Stuart had never taken the necklace off, as he would be reminded of his father during moments of struggle. Standing beside Ima, he unlocked the necklace from the back and took the shimmering collar off. Holding it tight in his right hand, he held it out in front of Ima to see.

"Stu, was' dat?" Ima asked oddly, laying his eyes on the exquisite jewelry placed in Stuart's hand.

"Here, take it." Stuart replied.

Ima was hesitant and looked closely at the cross that was dangling from Stuart's fingertips. Taking too much time to decide whether to accept the necklace, Stuart instead put the cross in Ima's pants pocket, leaving Ima confused.

"It was a gift from my papa. I want you to have it. Papa tells me whoever holds it, God will protect forever and ever. Just keep it as a sign of friendship."

Ima pulled the necklace back out from his pocket and held the cross as tight as he could.

"I dun' deser' dis...," said Ima, as if he had been guilty of taking the precious band. The only Stuart could give was, "You will kneed it."

Chapter 6

"Throughout the centuries there were men who took first steps, down new roads, armed with nothing but their own vision." Ayn Rand

"X...Y...Z... Those are the *letters* of the alphabet. Now, try to say this word." Stuart said to Ima, as he pointed to some writings in a notebook. Sitting together on the sofa in the living room, Stuart was determined to teach his illiterate friend how to read and write. Claiming he won't go "anywhere in life without knowledge," Stuart decided to tutor Ima every day after school, so he can be able to follow the current events in the world.

"Dat's uh ... C...A...T... uh...." Ima mumbled, unsure of what he was going to say next.

"No, no, no, first of all, C-A-T is pronounced CAT; it sounds like bat, rat, fat, just like those words. Second of all, you can't say THAT with a D in front of that. It is T-H, *TH*AT. Now, you try it."

For the next few hours until sunset, they practiced with one another; letter by letter and word by word. For the first time, Ima was being taught how to speak and read, and soon enough, he was able to understand messages that were being thrown at him on the television screen. Outside, the sun finally went to sleep, as a dark blanket clouded over the sky with stars shining in different spots.

"Isn't YOUR mama COMING?" Ima asked, emphasizing specific words that he had learned that day. Stuart laughed a little as he was pleased with his friend's improvement.

"You're finally starting to get the hang of it, now! She should be here any...."

Suddenly, the creaking of the front door opening was heard in the living room. Stuart and Ima became silent, knowing that someone had entered the house.

"Who is that? Stuart baby, is that you? Is someone else, here?" Janice Scott yelled from a distance, still unaware of the unexpected guest in her home. Before Stuart could respond, she entered the living room and noticed her son, along with an African-American boy, sitting on the sofa staring right at her gloomy eyes. Holding plastic bags full of groceries, she dropped them immediately on the ground, causing the floor to tremble, her face turning grotesque.

"Stuart, who in heaven is this boy? This ... creature?" she muttered so reluctantly, even Ima was able to understand what she was saying word for word.

"Mama, meet Ima. He's a new friend of mine and ...." Before Stuart could continue, Janice grabbed her son by the shoulder and pointed at Ima, who sat on the sofa with a blank expression on his face.

"If that boy does not leave this house in one minute, you sure will not return, either!" his mother exclaimed. "I do not EVER want to see you with him, or any other man, woman, child, anyone of his sort. You understand?" Stuart gave his mother a slight nod, as he led the confused Ima to the front door. He grabbed the notebook from the living room table and gave it to Ima to keep. Before Ima walked out the door, Stuart reminded him, "Meet me tomorrow, same time, same place. Remember, do not tell anyone."

Ima quietly nodded, hoping to conceal himself from Janice who was furiously yelling to herself from afar. As Ima ran away in the darkness, Stuart attempted to run upstairs to his room and hide from his mother's outrage. Unfortunately, she stood right behind him as the door closed and brought him into the living room.

"Do you want yourself killed, Stuart?"

"What mama? What do you mean? He is my friend, and you can't change that!"

"NO! Boy, you stop roamin' around with that nigger, and you start playin' with your other friends who don't got dirt on their skin. Do you want what happened to your papa to happen to you? If that little boy's people find out about what's going on between you two...."

"MAMA! You don't understand, mama! We're tryin' to fix this. You may think I'm too young to know what's goin' on ... I've been watchin' the news, I've been readin' the paper, I've seen people fightin' and yellin' on the streets, I'm not a child no more."

"Well, becoming a friend with an enemy is not going to solve it, baby...." Janice replied, this time in a much mild tone.

"Just wait, mama. Everything's going to work out for the best." Stuart sprinted from the living room and upstairs to his bedroom. Before he went to sleep, he lay on his back and prayed.

"Dear heavenly father, I want to pray to you for help. Help for peace. Help for safety. Help that you will bring peace to not only this town, but to this country. God, I wanna pray for my friend, Ima. He doesn't get treated the way he should be, and I wanna ask that you look over him and over all the people in this world. Colored people, white people, everyone, God. I pray that you will bring another blessed day upon us tomorrow, and I pray all this in Jesus' name, Amen."

Chapter 7

"You're in the midst of a war: a battle between the limits of a crowd seeking the surrender of your dreams, and the power of your true vision to create and contribute. It is a fight between those who will tell you what you cannot do, and that part of you that knows – and has always known – that we are more than our environment; and that a dream, backed by an unrelenting will to attain it, is truly a reality with an imminent arrival." Tony Robbins

"ZZZ...ZZZ...," screamed the alarms from the clock, as the sharp noise resounded throughout Stuart's room. Stuart arose from his bed and prepared himself for the day ahead. It was the first time in almost eight years that he did not wake up wearing his father's necklace, as he felt something empty inside of him. Walking downstairs, he noticed that his mother had left for the diner unusually early.

Stepping into the kitchen, he found a note on the dining table that read, "Dear Stuart, After school today, do not come to the diner. Just come back home; there is no need to stop by. Love, Mama."

Taking the note, Stuart left home and walked to school all alone. Again, it was very rare for him to walk by himself, as he would usually travel to school with his friends, Marc and Rich.

This time, all he could think of was waiting for the school bell to ring, signaling the end of the day. As time passed by and the periods continued, Stuart could only focus on what was so important that his mother had to warn him from staying away from the diner.

Finally, the final bell rang, as he joined a barrage of students storming out of the school. Checking the clock outside of the school building, it read, "3:00." Stuart stood on the sidewalk outside of school with people scurrying left and right like a traffic jam. He pulled out his mother's note from his pocket and reread it. He took a deep breath and decided to walk towards the diner, going against his mother's judgment to fulfill his promise with Ima. About five minutes later, he entered downtown part of Birmingham, where the streets appeared to look the same as usual; cars honking their horns and customers on sidewalks.

"Hm, I wonder why mama warned me about coming, here...," Stuart thought, checking around to see if Ima had arrived earlier than expected. As Stuart finally approached the alleyway, he heard thumping footsteps and familiar voices coming from behind. Turning around, there they were again: Marc and Rich.

"What are you guys doing here, now?" Stuart asked in an aggravated way.

"We were just gonna stop by at your mama's place and get some lunch. Why are you here ... oh wait! I *forgot*! You came to see your little black friend of yours, didn't you?" Rich laughed sarcastically, as both he and Marc surrounded the smaller Stuart.

"Just leave me alone you guys; there's no need for this."

"There is no need for this? Heh, did you hear what he said, Rich? No need for this? I do think there is a need for *this*."

Marc answered back. As both Marc and Rich were about to attack their former friend, they were disrupted by a strange chant coming from down the street. All three looked ahead and noticed a group of about twenty African-American people dressed in black march closer and closer towards them. It seemed as the customers on the sidewalks, and people coming from inside the stores along the street were noticing the rally. Soon enough, there was a massive crowd of men and women standing in the middle of the street; cars were forced to stop as on one side were all African-Americans and the other, the Whites.

Stuart was able to push his way towards the front to observe what was happening. The blacks dressed in black were standing approximately fifty feet away; almost all of them were dressed in similar attire. From a distance, Stuart couldn't recognize anyone, until he spotted one of the older men grabbing a boy similar in age with himself. Not one side budged nor made a sound, resembling a duel. For Stuart, he felt like he was in a dream; as if what was occurring at that moment was not happening in reality. Finally, he inched closer and closer to find out that Ima was standing on the other side of the street. He began to run towards him, but he was stopped when the old man grabbing his friend pulled out a weapon from his pocket. The weapon was too indistinct from far away, as Stuart stopped immediately. Loud grasps came from Stuart's side, as the many customers and observers were beginning to realize that a fight would break out any second.

"You! Stop!" yelled the old man, who looked very familiar to Stuart. He was trying to remember where he had seen this strange person, but at that moment, he couldn't afford to risk anything. "You, youngin', was' yo' name? ...en dun' move!"

Stuart could hear many people behind him trying to persuade him to move back and avoid any confrontation. At that moment, he felt like giving up and going back home, forgetting all of the dreams that he wished to come true. Another part of him was telling him the opposite; he knew that if he passé dup on this opportunity to unite the two conflicting "societies," the town would remain to endure more hardships and controversy.

"HIS NAME IS STUART! ST...," Ima yelled out desperately, as his mouth was then shut by what appeared to be his father's hand.

"You , shud up! I talk to da boy!" Ima's father replied, still holding the weapon, which appeared to be a small pistol, in his hand. "So, you da boy dat's bn' meetin' wit my kid, here?"

Right as his father asked the question, Stuart's heart sank rapidly. He could not believe that Ima had let the news of their secret friendship slip away. Suddenly, people from both sides began to chatter in bewilderment, never imagining something like this would happen. In rage, Ima's father let go of Ima forcefully, and dreadfully walked in front of Stuart, face to face. His smoky, brown eyes, and pungent garlic breath pinched nerves in Stuart's brain, as he began to shiver in fear.

"Dun' lie to me boy! Nah, you tell me, you ben' talkin' or doin' sumtin' I dun know with my chile?"

"Yes, sir."

More gasps were made, as both crowds gradually moved closer to the center. Ima was still lying on the ground from being thrown from his father.

"You ben' teachin' him sum lettas and readin'? ANSWER ME BOY!"

"Yes, sir."

With each response, the two enemy crowds began to inch closer and closer, as finally, Ima's father took his had and viciously slapped it across Stuart's cheek. Silence flew over the people, as Ima's father yelled, "NO ONE MOVE!" Stuart looked down, his teary eyes swelling up from the pain he had just suffered. He could feel the fingerprints imprinted on his soft cheeks; blood vessels in his skin bursting one by one like balloons. Suddenly, Ima stood up swiftly from the ground behind his father and ran towards Stuart to help him. At the moment Stuart looked up, he noticed from behind Ima's sprinting shoulders that his father was pullilng out his pistol from his pockt. All Stuart could do was yell.

"NO IMA, GET DOWN! NO!!!! DON'T SHOOT!"

The old man cocked his pistol back....

"STU! YOU ALRI...."

...and shot.

Stuart fell to his knees, as he watched his friend's eyes slowly shut in his arms. Before Stuart could move, he saw the gold cross hanging on his dying brother's neck.

Chapter 8

"The ultimate measure of a man is not where he stands in moments of comfort and convenience, but where he stands at times of challenge and controversy. The true neighbor will risk his position, his prestige and even his life for the welfare of others." Martin Luther King, Jr.

"You see, war is not the answer…. For only can conquer hate…," 24-year old Stuart Scott sang loudly along with the car radio. "Hey, mama, how's my voice? *To bring some lovin' here, today….*"

"Oh, it's lovely darling. You just singin' like papa used to back in the ol' days." Janice Scott chuckled. "Boy, you're just all grown up, aren't you?"

Stuart began to blush as he and his mother were driving back home after a l ong day at Scott's Pub. Although a short drive, Stuart decided to take a longer route this time, hoping to get some of the fresh, summer air with his aging mother.

"Ahh, 1980 … a new decade, a new start … mama, I think I'm getting' old!" Stuart proclaimed.

"Baby, you getting' old? I can barely walk, talk, hear, or do anythin' darling. It seems like you just graduated from high school!" Janice said in a very elderly manner. "By the way, where are you goin' honey?"

"I'm just gonna stop by at the Freeman's for a bit, if that's alright with you, mama."

"No, go ahead, tell them they won't be expectin' no apple pie this time!"

Stuart and his mother shared a quick laugh, as he drove down to the southern part of Birmingham. Whenever he would travel down to this part of town, Stuart was constantly reminded of that tragic moment, where Ima had sacrificed himself to save Stuart. Now, eleven years later, his childhood dream had finally come true; public facilities were open to the entire public, and transportation was permitted to all citizens. Ever since that day, the "Scott – Freeman Law," would be enforced on every building in Birmingham, as people of mixed color were now allowed to access any part of town.

Finally, Stuart and his mother reached the front of the Freeman house, which was located on a very small strip of farmland. The Scott family had bought this property for the Freeman's after Ima's death, and ever since, the two parties had become the best of friends. Stuart got out of his car and walked to the front of the Freeman's house. Knocking on their door, a young, beautiful, African-American girl, around the age of five or six, appeared from the window.

"Hello, who is this?" the girl asked in a high-pitched voice.

"Hi, I'm Stuart Scott. I'm Ima's brother. I just wanted to say hello and how you were doing?"

"PAPA! Someone's at the door!" the girl yelled, as there was wild commotion occurring from inside. Then, a very aged man, grey-haired with smoky skin, carefully limped towards the door on a cane. "Papa, his name is Stuart?"

"Oh yes, Stuart! It's Father Morgan. Come in!" the old grandfather gently opened the screen door, as it shut abruptly behind Stuart.

"Father Morgan, it's been years since we've last seen each other, how are you?" Stuart asked, aiding the old figure onto a rocking chair in their petite living room.

"Boy, you have grown so much. You're growin' some hair on yo' chin, I see? He he he, I hope you are doin' well. Sorry, my granddaughter be yellin' like a wild dog like that."

"No, it's ok, I just wanted to ask if I could leave something in Ima's room before I leave."

"You sure you don' wanna stay no longer, Stu?"

"I'm fine, Father Morgan. I'll be makin' my way upstairs. Thank you."

As Father Morgan quietly rested on the rocking chair, Stuart stood up from the sofa and walked up the wooden staircase to Ima's old bedroom. The door was closed shut; the doorknob covered in dirt and dust. Cautiously, Stuart turned the doorknob and entered the unoccupied room. The walls released its glimmering rays through the transparent windows, creating shadows on the wall. Posters of Hank Aaron dominated the walls, and the carpet on the ground was unblemished. The twin bed, enveloped in sheets of cotton, was perfectly organized from top to bottom; his mahogany, wooden desk holding notebooks and utensils. Stuart took a deep breath the moment he walked in, and took something out from his pants pocket. It was the gold cross necklace that was given to Ima eleven years back. He walked over to Ima's desk and placed the gold cross over Ima's self-portrait. Stuart couldn't hold back the tears, as he was able to feel Ima's pain at that moment swirl inside like a tornado. Before leaving the room one last time, Stuart found a small, loose-leaf paper hanging out from one of Ima's notebooks. Curious to see what was inside, Stuart read the letter, which said, "Stu, Thanks for helping me. Your friend, Ima."

Looking at the letter and the portrait, Stuart cracked a smile and looked up to the sky.

"Ima, life is not the same without you here. I only wish that you would have taken my life instead of your own. I miss you so much."

With each teardrop that fell onto the letter, Stuart was able to hear Ima speak back to him from heaven. The only words he could hear were, "Keep on, brother. Keep on."

Stuart looked back up once more and closed the door.

"Korean Americans vs. African Americans"

By Brian Lee (10th Grade, Plainsboro, NJ)

The first Korean immigrants arrived in Honolulu, Hawaii in January 13, 1903, on the SS Gaellic, a U.S. merchant ship. There were 101 Koreans on the ship: 55 men, 21 women, and 25 children (Hurh 31). The reason why the first Korean immigration happened was that Hawaiian sugar plantation owners needed cheap labor and Koreans were willing to work for prices that were lower than demanded by other peoples (Hurh 36). Since then, many more Koreans immigrated to the United States, and now there are nearly two million Koreans in the United States. Although there aren't too many Koreans working on sugar plantations now, Korean-Americans are involved in integral parts of American economy. And Korean-Americans are an important part of the economic supply and demand system. This is evident for anyone who has been to the local dry cleaners in major cities of America. Many Koreans manage dry cleaning businesses, but dry cleaning is not the only area of Korean economic focus. There are Korean fruit stores coloring the city of New York, and there are Korean grocery stores in Los Angeles. Often, Koreans manage stores in rough areas in economically depressed parts of major cities, like LA and NY. Predominate clientele has been African Americans. So it may not be surprising that there have been many conflicts between Korean Americans and African Americans. In this essay, I will discuss the conflict between Korean Americans and African Americans in NY and LA. Then, I will give my analysis and suggestions on the whole issue of interethnic conflict between African Americans and Korean Americans.

In New York, and many other places in America, there is an interracial conflict between Koreans and blacks. The tension between these two ethnic groups is somewhat different in different parts of America. And this is the case in NY as well: there is a distinctiveness to NY's interethnic conflict between African Americans and Korean Americans that sets it apart from those in other parts of America. In NY, specifically, Korean stores have experienced boycotts led by African Americans. In NY, the tension between Koreans and African Americans are based on what African Americans believe is Korean racism against African Americans, and blacks exploit this to gain political power over Koreans and for themselves in the wider American context.

Korean stores in NY were boycotted because the African Americans felt disrespect and racism from the Koreans. On January 18, 1990, a conflict broke out at a Korean owned fruit and vegetable store in Church Avenue in Brooklyn, New York. And it was this conflict that was the cause for what is known as "Church Avenue Boycott" by African Americans. Supposedly, Haitian immigrant, known as "sister Jhislaine", was beaten by three Korean merchants (Kim, 99). This led to a series of boycotts. These boycotts were meant to protest against the "racism of Koreans", but in actuality, these rallies, organized by groups of black nationalists like the December 12th Movement and Black Men's Movement, were used to gain political power for the African Americans in general and for their groups' political status. This explains for instance the involvement of Al Sharpton's and Sonny Carson's groups (Kim, 102). The conflict helped black activists and black entrepreneurs to show their interests and influences on urban America. The black community used these boycotts to take stronger control of their economic life. In the flyers distributed in the Church Avenue boycotts, flyers raised the question, "Who is going to control the economic life of the Black community?" (Kim, 99). Professor Heon Cheol Lee states, "The conflict situation related to Korean merchants and their business in black neighborhoods provided black activists and black political entrepreneurs with good political opportunities to promote their own interests and enhance their own political influence in urban America" (Kim, 99). So, it is not surprising that some Korean merchants felt that African Americans were being racist against Koreans and manipulating the situation just because the merchants were Korean immigrants. Many believed that the conflict between Korean Americans and African Americans in NY would not have happened without organized boycotts established by political groups in the African American community, which were national in nature. Professor Heon Cheol Lee states, "Without an organized boycott of Korean stores, there would be no black-Korean conflict in the form of direct, overt, collective actions (Kim, 92). Thus, the NY conflict between Korean Americans and African Americans can be seen as artificially generated by black politicians and business leaders who wanted economic and political benefits.

Black-Korean conflict in Los Angeles was different from the conflict in New York. Two victimized ethnic groups were in conflict, and the blacks' anger led to the devastation and destruction of Korean Stores. Unlike New York, where there was no destruction of Korean property, in LA there was a destruction of Korean property and possessions. Furthermore, in New York the conflicts were artificially generated by African American leaders, but in LA the conflict was spontaneous and involved mob violence against Korean Americans.

In Los Angeles, the African American civil unrest against Korean Americans in 1992 can actually be attributed to a verdict of innocence for white police officers who beat Rodney King, an African American man. It was right after this "not guilty" verdict, that African Americans started to attack businesses in South Central Los Angeles. Hispanic Americans were opportunistic in joining the looting of local Korean American businesses (Kim, 17).

The urban riots as a whole in LA won the most destructive urban riots in the United States. During this unrest, 58 people died, 2,383 were injured, and over 17,000 were arrested. The total property damage came out to be between $785 million and $1 billion. 4,500 businesses were totally or partially destroyed, in which 2,300 were Korean stores in South Central Los Angeles, where the poverty, crime, drugs, and the feelings of anger and despair rooted the LA unrest.

The reason for LA civil unrest can be seen as two victimized groups being confined to one local area. African Americans were discontent at what they perceived to be discriminatory treatment of blacks by whites and white structures in America. When the court system found white people who beat Rodney King "innocent", African American sense of victimization grew into a big fire that started to burn. Since the nearest targets were Korean American businesses in South Central LA, African American rioters attacked them. White businesses were too far away to attack and burn down. Many white businesses do not want to be in African American communities because there tend to be high crime rate, fewer people with high paying jobs, and "rude" low class consumers. However, Korean Americans, because they are immigrants, are willing to take the risk and the "rudeness" of African American neighborhoods. Thus, Korean American merchants fill a gap in the American economic system by providing business services to poor African Americans and Hispanic Americans. In this sense, Korean Americans play the "middleman minority role" (Kim, 28-31). Professor Kwang Chung Kim and Shin Kim states, "By running a business in inner-city ghetto areas and distributing goods purchased from white-dominated corporations and Third World manufacturers, these Koreans are inevitably placing themselves in the position of middleman minority, whether they are aware of it or not" (Kim, 30). Thus one sees that Korean immigrants are valuable to African American communities which have been abandoned by white merchants. However African Americans often do not see these Korean American businesses as rendering a valuable service for their communities. Often Korean American businesses become targets of African American discontent directed at whites. Professors Kim state, "Korean businesses were also somewhat more tempting targets than other businesses, because their culturally and racially different owners made them more visible and they had clearly proliferated in the area" (Kim, 33). Thus we see that Korean Americans and African Americans are victims in the Los Angeles conflict.

However, Korean Americans are more of a victim because they are attacked while providing services to African Americans which white Americans have abandoned.

What makes Koreans a double victim is that they are victimized also by the predominately white media that blame Korean Americans for the conflict in an effort to divert African American anger against whites. The white media refused to give voice to Korean community leaders on national television and often interviewed angry African Americans who blamed Korean American merchants on national TV. This not only gave the impression to most Americans that Koreans were guilty, it further inflamed African Americans against Korean American merchants. There is a reason why LA riots lasted several days: the white media fueled the conflict. Professor Kyeyoung Park states, "Whether the media blame the conflict on race or culture, their coverage is ahistorical. They further racialize black-Korean tension by conveying black intolerance of Koreans, which fuels the biases of Korean merchants, and their further contribute to Korean's negative portrayal of blacks through their use of stereotypical images" (Kim, 69). We still see the white media playing Korean Americans against African Americans.

When we examine the case of LA and NY we see a commonality in the midst of differences. The common factor is that Koreans are victimized and that African Americans play the primary role of the victimizer, whether instigated by black political leaders or by the white media. In NY, prominent African American leaders and black political and economical organizations boycotted Korean American merchants in order to empower themselves. In LA, African Americans looted Korean American Stores because they were angry at the white court system and the white social institutions that mistreated them, in their opinion. The white media fueled their anger and played a role in the destruction of Korean businesses.

What the similarities of the two cases show us is that Korean Americans have been victims of the victims. Koreans are victimized by those victims who want to vent their angers at their victimizers (in the case of African American communities, this would be white institutions). African Americans are often afraid to vent their anger at the dominant white society, so they end up picking on more helpless Korean American communities. Many Korean American merchants are immigrants from Korea who have not fully assimilated into American life and do not understand American society completely. Thus, Korean American businesses are highly vulnerable in the conflicts between Korean Americans and African Americans. What I see as a solution to this problem is to create Korean American leaders who understand American society and are capable of defending the Korean community both against political and economic attacks of African Americans and against the manipulations of white media that want to deflect African American anger toward vulnerable Korean American merchants and communities.

Bibliography

Hurh, Won Moo. *The Korean Americans*. Westport: Greenwood, 1998.

Kwang Chung Kim (Editor). *Koreans in the Hood*. Ed. Baltimore: Johns Hopkins University Press, 1999.

"My Church Called the Praise Church"

By Brian Kim (10th Grade, Belle Meade, NJ)

My name is Brian Kim, and I am a Korean-American who lives in Somerset County in a little city of Belle Meade. I attend Montgomery High School, and some of my interests include playing lacrosse and violin. And I am a part of the praise team that leads praise during youth services at one of the biggest Korean-American churches in New Jersy, Praise Church. I will describe to you my leadership role in my church and give you a picture of a Korean-American teenager is like in the context of the Korean-American church.

In order for the praise team to be prepared for Sunday worship service, our praise team meets every Saturday at 3 PM to practice. Our practice begins with a short Bible study among the team for fifteen to twenty minutes. Our leader, Jon (12th grade), comes to church with a Bible passage that may help the praise team. We discuss the passage together and pray as we close the Bible study. Then, we go into our instrumental practice. Since we have two praise leaders, Joe (11th grade) and Jon (12th grade), we decided to let them lead in alternating months. We have three electric guitar player, named Jeff (12th grade), Aaron (11th grade), and me, and we rotate every week so everyone gets a chance to play on Sunday.

During our instrumental practices, we first begin with either discussing about what son to play or just look over the songs that are already chosen by our leader. We usually pick about four to five songs. I think that one of the most popular songs that we play is called, "From the Inside Out," by Hillsong United. Whenever we sing this song, we can see the whole youth group being into the music, singing out loud.

On Sunday mornings before the praise team goes into actual service, we run through the songs we practiced before we perform. After we are done going over all the songs, we leave the Youth group service room and go into a quiet place for us to pray. We pray about our preparedness, our youth group, and about praising God with all our hearts.

After we are done praying, we go back up on stage and wait until our youth pastor is finished opening up the service. When it is our turn to lead the worship service, the leader will say a short prayer, and we start to perform. During our performance, we don't just sing through all four or five songs, but, sometimes, in between the songs, the leader will say few words of reminders and encouragement. At the end of the fifth song, we pray and join the youth group in service.

I was in the praise team ever since I was in seventh grade, and I have never regretted committing myself to participate in the praise team. Since all the other members started in their middle school year, too, we were able to grow up together and become closer to each other because of this team. We learned to respect each other and are able to take care of one another when someone is in need.

One of the biggest changes we all have seen within our praise team is that not only did we grow in friendship and in music performance, we grew more spiritually. We were only able to see this after we finally found a professional praise leader/pastor named Neah. She came to our church in 2007, and we learned a lot from her. She taught us how to lead great worship and to grow spiritually. Looking back at my early years of praise team, I feel I just did it without heart and full commitment, but now I realize that I need to take this opportunity, seriously. Thanks to our praise team pastor, we were able to learn to become great worship leaders.

Because I'm always up in front of the youth group every week, I get a chance to observe our youth group and what they do during worship, their personalities, etc. Our youth group is composed of a lot of youths coming from different areas. Many come from the area in New Brunswick, Princeton, and Bridgewater. We also have youths coming from as far as New York. They each have different personality, and from that we can learn about different Korean youths coming from sundry areas.

The kids in the youth are mainly nice and always wanting to take challenges. Because of their strong belief in Christianity, our youth group has seen a lot of changes over the few years. Since 2006, we took big steps in order to grow more spiritually. That started the preparation for the missions trip to New Orleans.

Unlike other missions, we took it very seriously to prepare for it very strictly. We had meetings twice a week and had Bible study for 2 hours, every meeting. The kids who were able to handle it were the ones that got to go. Some dropped out, but many stayed because they wanted to grow. An example of the rigorous program is missions leader Joanne making us run couple of miles to test our endurance. It was very hard, but many of the youth members and myself pushed ourselves to grow. We also practiced during some construction work because this New Orleans missions trip involved mostly construction work.

Finally, we went to New Orleans with a large group of 35 members of the youth group. We took an airplane from Philadelphia to New Orleans. It seemed like we filled half the plane, since it was a small plane. When we were there at the site we were going to work at, we were all blown away by what we saw. It has been 2 years since the disaster, and all we saw were broken houses and people just standing outside their ruined homes because they didn't have anything to do. Having seen enough of it, we went to the place where we were going to sleep. When we were there, there was another white church youth group from Florida waiting for us. For a week, we were to sleep and eat with them. Presbyterian Church (USA) sponsored the trip, and several denominational churches sent their youth members. We were the only Korean church represented.

What I learned from the missions trip was that I have too much "stuff" that I really don't need. The kids in New Orleans are living with nothing, but they are even happier than us who have all the stuff we don't need. I also learned that having everything doesn't bring happiness and that truly only having God in your heart will bring you true happiness.

As part of the praise team, I want to continue helping and guiding the youth group grow more spiritually. Also, I want to help the whole youth group realize what I learned – that materialism will only bring them short happiness but that putting away those materialistic things and focusing on God will bring them everlasting happiness.

"Emancipation to Benefit the White Man"

By John Baek (10th Grade, Closter, NJ)

The American civil war is often seen as a moral struggle to free slaves, but this may be a simplistic perception. It wasn't simply the fact that northerners wanted to free slaves and southerners did not want to free slaves. It is simplistic to say that the northerners were more moral then southerners in terms of treatments of slaves, or black people. In the north, in fact, blacks were treated worse than slaves in the south. As Leon F. Litwack states, "Until the post-civil war era, in fact most northern whites would maintain a careful distinction between negroes legal protection- a theoretical right to life, liberty, and prosperity- and political and social equality" (Litwack 15). Thus one sees that northerners viewed blacks as inferior to whites even though they had emancipated them.

There were many practices in the north that testify to their perception that blacks must remain inferior to whites. So, the emancipation of the north can be seen as not a morale decision on the part of most northerners but as a decision to benefit the white populace of the north. This is clear from such movements such as colonization that took hold in the north far strongly than in the south. Southerners had slaves leading up to the civil war, but often southerners treated their slaves better than the way northern whites treated freed blacks in the north. In fact, some southerners argued that it was moral to have slavery because northerners treated freed slaves so harshly and pushed them to economic degradation.

The northern states wanted there to be a clear distinction between both the white man and black man. The white man was supposed to be superior to the black man and many Negroes were brainwashed into thinking it was true.

To establish the difference between the white man and the black man, congress did not grant Negroes their full rights, even saying that negroes were not supposed to be under the word "citizens" in the constitution. Also, since there was no mention of race or color in the constitution, it was up to the states and the federal government to define their legal status, and many acted out of their hated Negroes. They also seized every moment possible to degrade negroes lower and lower.

The only reason why the slaves were freed was because it helped the white man. It was just cheaper to pay someone to get the job done instead of paying for a man or families worth of food, clothing, and shelter. It is important to recognize that one of the reasons for emancipation of blacks in the north after the revolutionary war was due to the fact that white day laborers complained. White day laborers complained because they did not have jobs. They attributed their unemployment to the fact that there were black slaves in the north. These white day laborers argued that if there weren't slaves, that they would have employment. But because there were slaves, white slave owners were not interested in hiring white day laborers. So these white day laborers pushed for emancipation of blacks in the north so that they could get employment in the north.

Ironically slave owners in the north wanted to free the black slaves in the north was well, but for a different reason.

Many slave owners found slaves costly to maintain. They had to feed whole families of slaves, including dependents who provided no helpful service to the slave owner. It is important to remember, that unlike the south, the north was going through an industrial revolution whereas the south depended on slaves for farming and agricultural output, northerners were beginning to become more dependent on manufacturing and production, which required more specialized skills. Black slaves were uneducated and unskilled workers who can do farmwork but could not be easily fitted to specialized labor. So, many black slave owners wanted to free black slaves so that they could have the capital to hire white day laborers who were better educated and could provide more specialized skill labor for white manufacturers. Thus, there was a convergence of interests to free emancipated black slaves in the north. It is clear that more northerners freed slaves for their own personal gain, rather than out of moral responsibility.

One sees that the northerners did not really care for blacks in the way the freed blacks were treated afterwards. Often, New England states refused to allow blacks to practice their rights as citizens. So even though emancipated blacks should have been allowed to participate in the political process, white political leaders as well as white citizens of the northern states often tried to bar them from participation. Furthermore, there were massive beatings of blacks in the north after emancipation. Whereas during the slave days slave owners might have beat their own slaves in the emancipated north it was fair game to beat any freed black. No white policeman was going to jump at the opportunity to arrest whites who beat up on blacks because that would have made them immensely unpopular in pro-white, anti-black New England leading up to the civil war. Thus it is not surprising that there were black slums created all over New England. Many blacks became unemployed as they were muscled away from legitimate jobs. Ironically enough, this had a snowballing effect of anti-black sentiment in the north. Not only did those without much negative sentiment against blacks come to think of blacks as dangerous elements. In their pure new England society, even those who had supported blacks in honest earnestness began to doubt themselves as formerly well-meaning whites looked at blacks who filled slum areas and behaved in a manner they perceived to be "very rude", they began to regret pushing for emancipation of blacks. Thus, whites who had fought to free black slaves began to say that they now realized that blacks were inferior and freeing them did not do anything to improve them. In essence, it was after the emancipation of the blacks in the north that they began to see as innately inferior.

It is clear to see that blacks in the north were perceived by the whites in the north as a problem. Especially after the emancipation, whites did not like blacks in the north and argued that emancipation was evidence for white support of blacks as misleading. Joanne Pope Melish states "This mythology lies at the heart of a second great misconception challenged by this work: that any responses of whites to free people of color in the north in the antebellum period were really 'about' southern slavery." (Melish 7). Northerners did not free blacks because they wanted blacks to be free or because they thought blacks were equal to them. Majority of the people wanted to free black slaves for their own gain. This is even clearer when we see the movement to colonize blacks in Africa.

Pro-colonization movement sprang up all over the north in the early 1800's, in order to create a white-only New England. Whites in the north did not even want to see black people in their cities. That is how much many whites in the north leading up to the civil war hated black people. They thought the best solution to the black problem was to expel all blacks to a colony created just for blacks. In contrast, southerners were not so hateful of black people. Southerners owned black people but they often saw black people and treated black people as part of the family. In fact often blacks were used as baby-sitters of the children of the master. Southern slave owners had no problem with black slave women touching their babies, and becoming like an aunt to them. This reality is best captured in the movie, Gone with the Wind.

Of course it is simplistic to say that all southerners treated blacks as part of the family. Many slave owners in the south were abusive of their slaves. However it would be doubly wrong to say that slave owners in the south were necessarily harsher in their treatment of blacks then the way that the whites treated blacks. This just is not true even though it is part of our popular myth. However we are looking through the lens of the conquerors in the civil war and are colored by their descriptions.

The civil war was not really about freeing the slaves, at least initially. The civil war was more about state rights vs. federal rights. Southern states wanted to practice their state rights and were willing to secede from the Union in order to preserve their state rights. President Lincoln at first was willing to let the south secede, but when he realized that it would endanger all of the Union, he became adamantly opposed to it. As Lincoln and the federal government fought to preserve the Union, the language of warfare took on more of anti-slavery argument. Thus, it can be argued that anti-slavery rational came after the pro-Union argument. One strong indicator of this was the fugitive slave law that was passed by the federal government. Less than ten years before the civil war, the US government was so interested in preserving the Union all the way up to the beginning of the civil war, that they were forcing northerners to return slaves to the south or face arrest and imprisonment by federal agents. In other words any northerner who refused to return a runaway slave back to the slave owner could be arrested and treated as a criminal by the US government all the way up to the beginning of the civil war. Thus we see that the federal government was more interested in preserving the Union rather than freeing the slaves in the south.

The American Civil War teaches our generation something about the realities of interethnic conflict. Joanne Pope Melish argues that the concept of "race" was an ideological construction that was created after the civil war based on the experiences leading up to the civil war, and that it was based on the construction of whiteness that was created because of "the problem" of freed slaves (Melish 5). In other words, Professor Melish as well as other scholars of ethnic studies and civil war historians argue that the color dividing line was only possible once black achieved freedom. Before the emancipation, blacks were non-persons. In other words blacks were not seen as humans in comparative terms. It was only possible to compare whites and blacks on an equal level after blacks became free. This shows us, that interethnic conflict is, to an extent, possible when the ethnic groups are in the same playing field.

It is with equal citizenship status that ethnic groups can engage in conflict of any sort. So, today's interethnic conflict should be understood in this light. It is because there is an assumed understanding of equality or equal status as citizens that different ethnic groups can compete with each other. In a sense, therefore, the reality of conflict, even violent conflicts, should be understood as possible because there is equality. Thus equality should not be seen as a solution to interethnic conflicts, in fact it is equality that engenders interethnic conflict. It is freedom and equality that creates conflict among the races and discord among different cultural groups in America. To a certain extent, we can argue that it is freedom that created interethnic conflict in Iraq. Without freedom and equal status there would not be the kind of violence in Iraq that exists today. Freedom may be a virtue and the value on a morale level, but it can not be denied that it is freedom that creates violence among different races and cultures. That is the very important lesson of the civil war.

Bibliography

"African American Troops in the Civil War, 1861-1865."
DISCovering U.S. History. Gale Research, 1997.
Reproduced in History Resource Center. Farmington
Hills, MI: Gale Group.
http://galenet.galegroup.com/servlet/HistRC/

Greeley, Horace. "Lincoln-Greeley Correspondence on Slavery
(1862)." 1862."Fugitive Slave Act (1850)." ABC-CLIO. 12
Nov. 2007
<http://www.usatwar.abcclio.com/Research/Display.as
px?entryid=768239&searchtext=northern+slavery&subc
ategoryid=46&total=158&ratio=1301&bc=new&nument
ries=34>.

Litwack, Leon F. *North of Slavery.* Chicago: University of Chicago
Press , 1961.

Melish, Joanne P. *Disowning Slavery.* Ithaca: Cornell University
Press, 1998.

Lowance, Jr., Mason I. (Editor). *A House Divided.* Princeton:
Princeton University Press, 2003.

"Educational Problems in Korea in Light of Korean History"

By Paul Park (9th Grade, Old Tappan, NJ)

Korea is a peninsula located in the Pacific between China and Japan. Korea is the only current "separated nation" under a political line. However, just like Germany, Korea wishes to reunite itself peacefully. Korea has 5,000 years of history starting with Ko-Chosun (3,000 B.C. to 4,000 B.C.). Korean mythology states that the son of god, Hwan-woong, came to earth to peacefully govern the people. The nation prospered, and two animals, tiger and a bear, came before Hwan-woong wishing to become humans. Hwan-woong instructed that they should eat worm-wood and garlic for 100 days, and they would become humans. Impatient tiger gave up but the bear waited and became human. The bear became known as Woong-nyu who married Hwan-woong. They had a baby named Dan-Goon who is believed to have established the first country on the peninsula, Ko-Chosun.

Around 4th century A.D., Korea enters the era of Three States. The peninsula was divided into countries, Kokuryo, Shilla, and Backje. These countries fought for numerous years and was finally united by Shilla. Over numerous land disputes, in 1392, the whole country gets united into Chosun, the last monarch empire in Korea. During the period of Chosun, one of the greatest kings of Korean history, King Sejong, contributes primarily in developing Korean economy, culture, technology and many more.

To get a deeper understanding of the Korean culture, we need to observe the life and the achievements of King Sejong. King Sejong was the third son of King Taejong, the 3rd king of the Chosun Dynasty in Korea. King Taejong had three sons who were Yangnyung, Hyoryung, and Choongnyng, or known as King Sejong. As a young kid, King Taejong favored King Sejong over his brothers. King Taejong had thought that his third son, King Sejong was the most appropriate for the throne. However, because King Taejong himself killed his brothers to get the throne, he has decided to appoint the first son as the King. But contrary to his expectations, Yangnyung was not really suitable as the king. So, Yangnyung intentionally acted rudely in the court, and was finally banished from the throne. So, King Taejong appointed King Sejong as the king in 1418.

King Sejong primarily thought that cultivating talents was the most important. So King Sejong established and expanded the Jib-Hyun Jun, or the Jade hall, and allowed the brightest minds of the country to study. King Sejong also wanted his people to read. As a result, King Sejong began to develop a concise, aligned type faced in order to print and distribute books to his citizens in 1434. This was 10 years ahead of the metallic typeface created by Gutenberg in Germany. With such an invention, he helped publish numerous books such as Hyohang ryok, Samgang hang sil do, Nong sa jik sul, and many more. Not only books, King Sejong contributed a lot in inventing other useful clocks. King Sejong appointed low class slave to a high position who later invented different types of clocks using water, sunlight, and stars.

Out of all his contributions, the most important contribution was the invention of Hangul, the Korean Native alphabet.

After he became the king, King Sejong realized that the low class citizens could not read, for the letters used at that time was Chinese. Chinese letters are hard to learn because they consist of more than 5,000 characters in which every single character have their own meaning. So, unless one was a high class of the society, it was truly hard for the citizens to learn how to read. So, King Sejong decided to create a new efficient and easy readable letters for his people. He established the Jib Hyun Jun or so called the Jade Hall, in which he gathered the brightest minds of the country to together create and assemble new language for the Korean people. In 1443, King Sejong published the volume of books named *Hunmin Chongum*, literally meaning proper sounds for instructing the people, which taught the people of Chosun its new letters. These letters or more conveniently called Hangul, is not an imitation of ancient letters or other characters but an alphabet unique to Korea. These letters, Hangul consist of 18 consonants such as ㄱ,ㄴ,ㄷ,ㄹ,ㅁ,ㅂ,ㅅ,ㅇ,ㅈ,ㅊ,ㅋ,ㅌ,ㅍ,ㅎ and 14 vowels such as ㅏ,ㅑ,ㅓ,ㅕ,ㅣ,ㅡ,ㅜ,ㅠ,ㅐ,ㅔ,ㅗ,ㅛ. Korean letters are scientifically proven to be designed based on the bone structure or the movements while pronouncing these sounds, and they are also very easy to learn. For example, English letters *n* and *d* have the same mouth structure. They both touch the ceiling of your mouth. However, they do not have any common trait visual wise. However, Korean letters ㄴ and ㄷ equivalent to the sound of *n* and *d*, both look alike and sound similar. Also, Korean word is a combination of the letters mentioned above. For example the word, 한, is a combination of the consonant ㅎ vowel ㅏ and consonant ㄴ. Korean unlike the English Alphabet is an accurate letter system even adding phonemic structural characteristics. Jeffery Sampson stated that Korean was "a qualified lettering system" (Kim 181). Hangul's efficiency is once again proven by being included in UNESCO's World Cultural Heritage in 1997. In short, King Sejong's invention of Hangul is very well known for its efficiency and its scientific structure.

King Sejong is probably the most important historic figure Korean history has ever produced. King Sejong's accomplishments not only shine because they are great but because it's from his pure sincere heart that was always for his people. King Sejong's great accomplishments still shine until now. In the early 1900s, Chosun ends by being occupied by the Japanese for 36 years.

After Hiroshima and Nagasaki was bombed, Japan surrendered and Korea also gained its independence. After Korea gained independence from Japan in 1945, Korea had a domestic conflict whether to set the government in a Communist society or a Democratic Society. Korea, not being able to conclude which doctrine the country's going to follow, was split up in 1945 by Russia and the U.S. Russia took control over North Korea and US took power in South Korea. Although through such hard times, Korean people have struggled to become one of the prominent nations in about 50 years, and since that period between 1950 and 1953, South Korea has never looked back.

Korea was not Republican society from the start. There were numerous autocratic presidents, like Seung-Man Lee and

Jung-Hi Park. Lee ruled for 8 years, and Park was the president for 18 years. However, due to strong protest, Lee resigned during his fourth term, and Park was assassinated after 18 years of dictatorship. Ever since, Korean presidents had 2 terms maximum setting a country in a more democratic society. However, through such dictator like presidents, the Korean economy has been boosted crucially.

The GNP (Gross National Products) per Capita of an individual has risen $4,000 during the past 30 years. Korean electronics, car, and shipbuilding are dominant in the global market. Although Korea is a packed country having 14,000 people in a square kilometer, Koreans developed their own way of living from the best of what's given.

Although Korea is dominant in electronic products, their companies are very limited in number. Just like the monopoly system, companies like Samsung and LG, have a grip in the market so the entrepreneurs are reluctant to start a new business. Also, Jae-bul, the tycoons, in Korea own many companies. So, one person owns quite a number of different companies, hiring their family or friends to a high position. Unlike America where there are lots of resources and new ideas to develop, Korean business market is very limited. So, the tycoon system limits the wealth to selective top class.

Differing from South Korea, North Korea has many other resources and positive factors Korea lacks. For example, they have tourism resource, vast empty land and when united, it will be a new country transitioning Korea to other foreign countries like China and Russia. However, the North Koreans are under a communist dictator, Kim Jung-Il. Majority of the citizens are not given any sort of pay and not fed. Also, because of the famine that's been going on for numerous years, millions of

North Koreans including babies and women are dying. So, South Korea and the UN have been supplying food and other supplies.

Because Korea is divided, it limits the potential of both countries to expand. First of all, as a result of having a big population in a small space, there are many competitions. College education is necessary in order to carry out a middle classed life. Also, because of the Confucianism that has been planted in the country for more than a millennium, Korean way of thinking was afflicted also. Confucianism idea has been came from China, invented by a scholar named Confucius. Confucianism focuses more on respect and way of getting along with each other, instead of having an intellectual being that controls the world. The five cardinal relationships theme in Confucianism are ruler to subject, father to son, husband to wife, older brother to younger brother, friend to friend. They value these relationships and a form of respect is necessary between the relationships. Also, Because of the Confucian idea of effort and achievement, an individual is not valued unless accompanied by a good profile

One of the problems relating to education is in the competition of going to a college. Unlike America, Korea has limits for a lot of things. For example, they have only so many companies to work in, and only so many colleges that provide good opportunities to be hired under a good company. So many students compete to exceed others. In October, senior students take the national test called "Soo-neung." Since this test determines which college they are going to go to, numerous companies start later in the test day in order to reduce the traffic for the students. On the other hand, American people do not do anything on the day of the SATs. This reflects the difference in values between America and Korea. Korea is a Confucianism society whereas Americans see education as peripheral or not as important as other elements like business and politics. Even though many companies yield to those who take the tests, the test is tough and harsh for the students. Soo-neung has 5 subjects on the test which include Korean, math, world language, science, and social studies. It starts at 9 am in the morning and ends at 4 p.m. This test, Soo-neung, unlike the SATs, you can only take it once a year. So many students, who failed to go to a good college, needs to wait another year to take the test. Since a good college is necessary to get a good job, many students compete to go to a good college such as Seoul National University, Korea University, or Yonsei University.

From the short interview with Seung-Min Lee who is now attending Yonsei University, I could learn more about the school system in Korea. He has told me that everything basically gets decided at the end of junior high school. After middle school, students take tests which divide them into three different high schools. One is Teuk-Mok Go, these are considered the best high school. If one attends this school, their chance of going to the best colleges in Korea is 76% compared to In Moon where around 5% go to top colleges. So, ranked 100th in Teuk Mok Go has a better chance of going to Seoul National University than ranked 1st in In Moon Go.

The next category which is In-moon is in the middle of the school levels. These are students probably aiming for some Jee Bang or country side colleges, or some low ranked universities in Seoul. The bottom of the high school chain is Sil Up Go. This high school consists of variety of students. This high school has the purpose of giving kids the opportunities of working right after high school for example in factories or banks. It usually consists of kids with financial problems or who are very far from the word "study." Besides these colleges there are few more. For example, there is Che Go, which is for students who are looking forward to playing sports at a national or an international level after college, and Ye-go for kids with art talents. Thanks to Seung-Min Lee, I have a deeper understanding of Korean high schools.

Besides the rigid structure of Korean secondary school education, another problem for Korean education is in the mentality of the companies. The companies only think about the benefit of themselves rather than a long term investment for the country. So companies, for example, give scholarships to the smartest people but do not invest in students with financial problems. So, the companies only invest in students for the good of the companies. And of course, none of the wealthy tycoons invest in building a new college either, causing many competitions. Unlike Carnegie-Mellen University and other colleges in America, there has not been a single college built by donations of a tycoon. And since there are only so many universities the companies recognize, it is truly hard for the graduates to find a good job. In short, it is a tragedy that a criterion for judging a person is based on their transcript rather than the sincerity or the potentials.

The third problem is the psychological pressure students receive during their high school years. For example, 14,000 high school students committed suicide during the year 2005, topping the most suicides in a year among OECD members (Organization for Economic Cooperation and Development). The amount of extra academies and tutors Korean students take is unbelievable. High school students are required to stay in school from 7 a.m. to 9 p.m. and they go to different outside studying places on the weekends. However, among those students less than 5% from accredited high schools go to top five schools in Seoul. And not only are the students worried about their future, the expectations of the parents' are high because of the emphasis on education. Also, Koreans have the perception that if a child goes to a bad college, there must be a problem with the parents. Because the Korean society is Confucian, one of the values of the parents is to invest to provide the children with the best education possible. Though history, Koreans have developed such a society value. So, the parents have high pressure because they want to keep their pride. In conclusion, the amount of work they put in compared to the number of students getting into good colleges is very discouraging. Hence, the pressure the society puts on the students about their future is another major problem.

Speaking of pressure, another short interview between Yeo-wool and me helped me understand about pressure in Korea. In Teuk Mok Go, high school students are required to stay in school until 9 p.m. for self studying. She has told me that it is called a voluntary study, but everybody has to stay. However, in In Moon Go, voluntary study is really voluntary, but only rank from 1 to 100 can get in. And since the classroom which holds the voluntary study has 100 desks with their names on them, sitting 1st on the top left seat to 100th on the bottom right seat. So, even if one wants to study, if he or she is not smart enough, they can't get in. Also, she told me that when she went to high school when she was young, the teachers based their class curriculum on the first 3 rows. In other words, approximately the first 3 rows actually studied and the others basically slept or did not pay attention. From such limited high school system, maybe it is obvious that the country's limited.

In conclusion, the education system in Korea is a major problem in the current generation. However, the competition has improved Korean Economy and the quality of life we have now. If it wasn't for the tight fight, Korea might have been one of a third country. So, it is perhaps very fortunate that the country is run by selective brightest and the elite class of the society.

"Uncle Tom's Cabin and Koreans"

By David Lee (9th Grade, Princeton, NJ)

Mr. Shelby is a farm-owner who owns a slave. This was very common in this book's time period. Uncle Tom, Eliza, and Harry were the most cherished slaves. By force, Shelby is forced to sell Harry and Uncle Tom (Harry is Eliza's son). Eliza, after eavesdropping on their discussion of the trade, runs away with the child. She is pursued by Haley, the slave-trader who wished to buy them. The desperate mother was helped by good citizens along the way. Unfortunately, Eliza is not the only one who receives help. Haley is aided by two other slave catchers. Tom, left behind, allowing the other two to escape, was taken away by Haley.

George Harris is Eliza's husband. He finds out of her escape towards Canada, and sets out to find and join her. Eliza and Harry are under the care of a good-hearted family at the moment. Luckily, George finds them. The married couple, along with their son and two other escaped slaves run while in pursuit by other slave catchers. When one is wounded by George's gun, the other slave catchers flee, and the wounded is brought along (due to Eliza's persuasion to treat him).

Meanwhile, Tom while on a boat meets a white girl, Eva St. Clare. Tom admired her beauty, and also rescues her from drowning. From doing so, her father buys Tom off of Haley. Eva and Tom form a strong relationship, and Eva grows fond of Christianity and begins to enjoy it. Eva writes to Eliza about Tom's well-being and location. But meanwhile, back in Ketucky, Aunt Chloe (Tom's wife) persuades Mrs. Shelby to be hired out to a confectionary baker in Louisville along with her money to buy their freedom.

A few years later, Tom realizes that Eva has a terminal illness. Her father is in denial from shock. But as Clare's condition worsens, the family accepts the horrible truth that Eve, indeed, was dying. She is mourned by all after her death. The father, influenced by Tom, follows the path of Christ and promises his freedom and protects all his slaves from being sold. Unfortunately, the father is suddenly killed, and the wife sells all of their slaves including Tom.

Tom's new owner is not so generous as the last couple he has had. Simon Legree, a plantation owner buys him, plus two other women for wrong reasons. While Tom is assigned to pick cotton, he meets Cassy, Legree's "concubine," and finds out of her horrible story. Tom, as gentle-hearted as he is, attempts to help his fellow slaves and whipped half to death. Legree actually vowed to either crush his spirit or kill him. Cassy, a very good soul, tries her best to save Tom, using her influence.

With Eliza, George, and Harry, they are fortunately able to cross over to freedom. However, it wasn't so pleasant with Tom. To describe Tom's heartache: he almost lost his faith in Christ. But Cassy, the angel, devises a way to escape with her intelligence, and Tom used his influence to encourage the other slaves to escape with them. But while doing so, Tom is caught. He was whipped and beat mercilessly. Mr. Shelby, when he decided he was going to sell Tom and Harry, vowed that he will return and buy Tom's freedom for certain, and he keeps his promise in the end. Unfortunately, Tom was dying away at the moment from all the beating and whipping, that Shelby was only just in time to hear his last words.

Cassy and the others have made their escape successfully, however, and meets George and Eliza on a boat headed somewhere north. Fascinating things happen here. Eliza just so happens to be Cassy's daughter! And one of the slaves who escaped along with Cassy, claims that she was George's sister. Shelby, as he was returning to the farm, notifies Chloe of Tom's influential death. Chloe was heartbroken from sadness and disappointment, of not being able to buy his freedom. Shelby, as a kind white slave-owner, frees all of his slaves and reminds them all that their freedom is the work of Tom's will.

Korean Americans are similar to the slaves in *Uncle Tom's Cabin* because Korean Americans are just like the slaves, except paid with a roof over their heads. They can many times suffer prejudice and be treated badly or unfairly. They work long hours without making as much money as they deserve. Family is something we have, and what the slaves were torn apart from. Even though we might not go through physical agony as the slaves did, but we can be hurt mentally and psychologically from racism or prejudice.

However, Korean Americans are at present may be less successful than blacks now. My vice principal is black, and I've never heard of Korean principals or almost any type of leaders for that matter. Blacks, in my opinion, probably have a strong will and extreme tenacity. Another example of a tenacious African-American leader is Toni Morrison of Princeton University, which is less than 10 miles from my home. Even in politics, there are many black leaders. For example, Condoleeza Rice is the United States Secretary of State. No Korean is at that level. Before becoming the Secretary of State, she was the Provost of Stanford University. And Brown University currently has a black president. In contrast, there are no Koreans who are presidents of great universities. This proves that blacks have achieved far more than Korean Americans.

Even in the business world, there are many black leaders making millions of dollars who are CEO's of major companies. As far as I know, there is not one major CEO of a US company who is Korean. Although average, Koreans live better than African Americans, the best African Americans have achieved greater status than the best Korean Americans.

Obama, a presidential candidate for the 2008 election is an African American who had studied in an Ivy League university. In the same Ivy League university, there are more Korean students than African American students, but blacks achieve far more. This is confusing to me. I feel that we Koreans must be doing something wrong, but I am not sure what that is. I'd like to break this pattern and achieve greatness as a Korean American. That's why I'm working very hard. I am currently memorizing20 SAT words per day and reading *Oliver Twist* by Charles Dickens.

I want to make my parents proud of me. My parents work very hard in their dry cleaner's. My dad works 16 hours, and often my mother works with him. I want to make my grandmother proud of me because she takes care of me and my sister, who is 2 years old.

I have to confess that I was almost moved to tears after reading *Uncle Tom's Cabin*, and I felt sad for those blacks who suffered in the past. However, I live in 2007, and know that Korean Americans are suffering more than African Americans. I am sure that *Uncle Tom's Cabin* inspired me to be better for my Korean community.

"Tradition and Lottery"

By Joon Park (9th Grade, Upper Saddle River, NJ)

In the short story, "The Lottery," by Shirley Jackson, a village of about three hundred people gathers for a lottery every year, conducted by Mr. Summers, a coal business owner. A pile of stones is placed in the corner of the square. Everyone attends the lottery, including children and even injured people. This is how the lottery is done: First, the husbands pick a slip of paper from the box. Then the winner's family each picks a slip of paper. Whoever chooses the slip of paper with a dot on it gets stoned by the village. The lottery is done because it has been performed by the village ever since it was established. However, some details of the tradition have been forgotten. Despite the lottery's importance to the village, there are attitudes of nervousness, the questioning of its fairness, and the doubt of its legitimacy.

Tradition can be the main reason why the village people choose to do the lottery. It is mentioned in the story that the lottery has been going on since the town started. It is also mentioned that the box used for the lottery has been made of parts from the original lottery box. This shows that the tradition of the lottery must be very important. The lottery must have been going on for a long time because it is explained in the story that the people forgot how the original lottery was performed. For example, one sees in page 2: "...some people believed that the official of the lottery used to stand just so when he said or sang it, others believed that he was supposed to walk among the people..." However, they still remember the core parts, such as heads of households drawing for their families and using stones to throw at the winner of the lottery.

There are several different attitudes towards the lottery that is repeatedly shown throughout the story, such as exhibiting of nervousness and the questioning of its fairness. Nervousness is repeatedly shown throughout the course of the story. In the story, Mr. Adams says, "They do say... that over in the north village they're talking of giving up the lottery" (page 4). This shows that he is nervous about the lottery, so he suggests discontinuing it. Another example of nervous attitudes towards the lottery is found in Mrs. Hutchinson's words, "Clean forgot what day it was" (Page 2). These words spoken to Mrs. Delacroix show that Mrs. Hutchinson is nervous because she is in a state of denial even when she stands with the townspeople for the lottery. Besides attitudes of nervousness exhibited throughout the story, questions regarding the fairness of the lottery exist throughout the story. Mrs. Hutchinson constantly raises the question of fairness. She accuses Mr. Summers of not giving her husband enough time. She says, "It wasn't fair!" (page 5). Again, she raises the question of fairness when she herself is chosen as the "winner" of the lottery. She screams, "It isn't fair, it isn't right" (page 6).

For the village in the story, "The Lottery," by Shirley Jackson, the lottery represented a long standing tradition that began since the founding of the village. The practice of the lottery continued annually without much questioning. However, there are traces of dissenting attitudes towards the lottery, exhibiting of nervousness, and the questioning of its fairness, and doubting of its legitimacy. Despite these attitudes, the story concludes with the stoning of the winner of the lottery, just like all the years passed.

After reading this story, I felt like certain traditions are bad. On the other hand, I don't want to be carried away by the exaggerated criticism of tradition by Shirley Jackson. Generally, traditions are not this cruel. Traditions are usually good ones that the community values and enjoys. I would like to steer away from the extremist criticism of Shirley Jackson, and I would like to argue that traditions are usually good. It is hard to find tradition as cruel as shown in "The Lottery." Despite the fact that I was tempted to stand against the concept of tradition after reading this story, I prefer to take a more moderate road and stand up for tradition. As a Korean-American, I appreciate many of the traditions that are in the Korean-American society. I feel Korean-American and I treasure my Korean-American identity, and so I treasure these traditions as a part of my identity.

"What I Think Korea Is Like"

By Gloria Bae (5th Grade, Closter, NJ)

I think Korea is full of apartments. There are probably a lot of food stands, and there are lots and lots of elementary, middle, and high school students. I have seen Korea on TV lots of times, but I've never been to Korea. When I saw Korea on TV, I saw that there are vineyards where you get to pick your own fruit. There are different kinds of fruit. There are grapes, apples, peaches, oranges, and more!

There is also Lotte World, I have been told. My friend went to Korea on summer vacation, and she told me that when she went to Lotte World, she almost fainted because there were so many rides to go on, and she only had a couple of hours. She said it was so much fun. Since then, I've always wanted to go to Lotte World.

I also saw on TV that they make very, very delicious foods, there. There are some unique foods, there, too. There was a walk-in store in Korea, where you got to pick a red, yellow, or green type of noodle. The red one was made out of *bo-ree-cha* (wheat tea), and the green one was made out of green tea. After you chose the type of noodle you wanted, the people would put that type of noodle in a clear plastig bag that doesn't leak, and they would pour this cold broth in the bag, along with the noodles. And then, you would go outside to eat the noodles. The line was really long, so it went all the way outside the walk-in. It was so cool. Actually, Korea is the place I always dreamed of going. I hope we can go to Korea, next year!

There are several holidays in Korea. First, there is *Goo-jung* or *Shul-nar*. It means "New Year." When it is *Goo-jung*, relatives from far way have a reunion. Mainly, people eat a traditional dish called *duk-gook*, made of rice cakes with meat inside in soup broth. If you eat it, you "grow one year older." There are other delicious foods, too. On *Goo-jung*, you wear *han-bok* (traditional Korean clothes which is very colorful), and the young people bow to their grandparents in a special rite to show respect. The grandparents give money to the people who bowed, as is the tradition. They encourage you.

Then, there is *Choo-suk*. It means "Thanksgiving." It's on 8/15 in Korea. The main food you eat is *song-pyun*, which is a rice cake with bean paste inside. Relatives also have reunions. Most people wear *han-bok*. There are lots of fruits and vegetables. Kids play *jae-ki-cha-ki*. It is a game where you throw the ball wrapped up in plastic feather up into the air and try to hit it with your foot.

Also, there is *Dae-bo-room*. It is the first day of the year that has a full moon. It is on 1/15 in Korea. You eat *oh-kok-bap*, a special kind of rice dish. There are five different kinds of grains in it. Kids go outside to do fireworks. For fun, everyone doesn't go to bed early because if you do, they say your eyebrows become the color white.

There is *Kwang-bok-chul*. A long time ago, for 36 years, Japanese people ruled over Korea. In 1945, 8/15, the Koreans were free. So, it is the Korean Independence Day. It is a national holiday.

Also, there is *Hyung-choong-il*. It is Korean Memorial Day. In 1919, 3/1, a 13-year-old girl was shouting, "Hooray for Korea!" over and over again. At that time, the Japanese were ruling over Korea. The girl was shot by a Japanese soldier and died. Her name was Yoo, Kwan-Soo.

"My Korean-American Journey"

By Esther Hah (12th Grade, Closter, NJ)

I was born on January 15, 1990, in Pusan, South Korea. Pusan is the second largest city in South Korea and is also the southern most city located on the southeastern tip of the Korean peninsula. Pusan is particularly known for its fishing industry and for producing many military leaders. In fact, President Chun and President Park both came from Pusan. Also, Pusan is the center of the Koshin Presbyterian Church denomination.

I am the first child of two daughters of Reverend Seung Maan Hah and Young In Hah. My parents were both born in Pusan, South Korea, and the three of us resided there until I turned 2-years-old. At the age of two, my parents decided to immigrate to the United States, specifically to Glenside, Pennsylvania. Glenside is where Westminster Theological Seminary is located. Westminster Theological Seminary is the seminary that was founded by Presbyterians who had helped to found my father's Presbyterian denomination in Korea.

Ever since we arrived to the States, my father's duty as a Reverend came first. There, we attended a church known as The First Korean Presbyterian Church in Philadelphia (FKPCP); evidently, church life dominated my life in all aspects whether it was home or school, given that I was raised in a strong Christian family. Nonetheless, we embraced our new lives even through adversity with strong determination and managed to live as comfortably as anyone in our position could live.

It was only a few months since we moved that a new member came to join the family; namely, my sister, Jeena ("Gin-ah") Hah. It was May 5, 1992, that I became an older sister and first realized that I would have responsibilities of my own. Ever since that day, as my life progressed, I finally began to grasp the concept of dependability.

As an older sister, it has always been my duty to look after my younger sister. Because I was more experienced in life than Jeena, my parents would often expect and remind me that it was important to act as a role model for her. More importantly, they believed that it was crucial for me to teach and help guide my naïve sister on to the proper path, which of course was Christianity. The fear that my mistakes and choices could ultimately lead to affect my sister was a risk I did not want to take. Thus, in my eyes, I had unfortunately often regarded my sister as somewhat burdensome rather than as a blessing.

As the two of us came of age, Jeena and I attended public schools together, until that is when I graduated from pre-school. I recall several memories from my very first elementary school, Glenside Elementary School; yet, one of my best experiences at Glenside was Wednesday lunch hours. Every Wednesday of the week, the school would hold a gift shop near the cafeteria. This was always one of things I would look forward to in a week because it was a time when I could buy something new and interesting. I remember how all the children would run toward the small table to get a glance of what new objects they could purchase that day. Electric yoyos, twirling lollipops, moon rings, and other funky objects would often be on display. Though some children may have considered Wednesday lunch hours as mere times of entertainment, to me, it strangely signified more. True, the objects on display were fascinating, but it helped me understand American culture in a sense. During the late 1990's, when Spice Girls and Britney Spears became the new and most important topics, I remember how the majority of the objects sold at the gift shop table were concentrated on these two pop artists. While everyone in the entire world seemed to be into them and knew everything about them, I personally knew nothing and felt alienated from the rest of my peers. Being that I was raised in a Christian home, anything that was secular was not permitted to me.

The fact that my parents were devout Christians was influential to the entire family. From the moment my sister and I were born, we were only exposed to Christianity and never anything that would arouse secular interests. According to my parents, anything secular related was considered tainted and immoral. When I was about 9 years old, I was given one of the most popular artist CD's, Nsync and A*Teens, by a relative of mine. Though in truth I knew they were secular, I could not resist the temptation to listen to them. All I wanted was to listen and enjoy my CD's so that I, too, could finally be a part of the norm in society. Yet, the second my parents discovered that I possessed them, the CD's were disposed of.

In a way, I suppose my parents were only trying to protect me from the corrupt world, but I cannot help but question whether they feared I was going to fall into the wrong path. Thus, the reasons for the number of Bible studies, discussions, not to mention, prayers my family and I would do. In fact, nearly all of my books were Christian related and hardly the typical American Babysitter's Club or any other. Every night, before bed, my sister and I were encouraged to make a prayer and read at least a verse from the Bible. Though it seemed only right, I recall how I became to loathe it.

These inner struggles that I had with Christianity, or what you may call rebellion, emerged during my late elementary years. Though I absolutely loved attending church, I was never too thrilled about being a Christian. In essence, I felt burdened by it. The fact that my father was a reverend greatly impacted me more negatively than positively. Like any PK, a term referred to as Pastor's Kid, I often felt overwhelmed due to the seemingly endless onerous responsibilities and expectations that were cast upon me. It was enough that I had to look after my sister 24/7, but now to expect an angelic, well-behaved, mannerly daughter, in the face of the public, never seemed to be adequately emphasized. "Just sit still and don't fuss," my mother used to say, or in front of others, sit still and don't talk. Even worse, it seemed to be imprinted on her forehead. Obediently, I did exactly that and would not even dare to move but force out a smile occasionally. I even recall times when my entire body would sometimes ache because of the long hours that I remained still. Evidently, just like any other child, I grew a hatred and impatience for it and ultimately rebelled.

During my elementary years in Glenside, Pennsylvania, my rebellion was basically internalized; but my contempt grew with each advancing year. It was when I moved to Closter, New Jersey, towards the end of my 6th grade, after two brief years spent in Bayside, New York, that my internalized rebellion took an externalized form. It was my middle school years in Tenakill Middle School that I began to succumb to worldly pleasures. Unlike my previous homes, Glenside, PA, and Bayside, NY, Closter, NJ, was a whole new different world. Never have I seen a town that was so clean, pure and friendly looking. However, its appearance proved to be the exact antithesis of what the town consists of. At first glance, I fell in love with the town. What this small, suburban town had seemed to be is exactly what I had hoped for. The house, the neighborhood, the stores, everything appeared to suit me. Best of all, many Koreans resided in this area. I was now finally able to befriend those who shared common backgrounds as me.

As years passed and I grew older, I became fond of secular materials more and more. Seemingly an innocent and pleasant town, Closter, in truth, was most corrupt out of all the places I have lived. It centralizes popularity, wealth, and outer appearance, all of which I was raised to disregard. However, the more I lived here and befriended my peers, the more I became exposed to worldly delights. As a matter of fact, it was in my middle school years at Tenakill that I grew to excessively take notice of my appearance. Never once have I have even bothered with the way I look or how I dress in public besides church related functions. Yet, now that I lived in Closter, my outer appearance climbed to be the top priority on my list. Little by little, I started to lean toward worldly possessions, first of which were books. The turning point of my life from my Christian upbringing to seeking secular materials was probably the moment I picked up my first controversial book; that is, *Harry Potter*. Eventually, other worldly topics attracted me and I grew submissive. Music, one of the most emphasized topics my parents would warn me about, now only seemed to be harmless and more importantly, fun.

Harry Potter may seem like a harmless book that has gained widespread popularity; however, those who closely observe the reactions of Evangelical Christians in America, who number at least 33% of the population, would have a strong reaction to it. Evangelical Christians reacted against Harry Potter making witchcraft fun and "cool." Although not buying into the harsh treatment of witchcraft in *The Crucible* by Arthur Miller, Evangelical Christians shared kindred spirits with those in opposition to witchcraft. Even to this day, many oppose such readings. Thus, one can see how my fondness in *Harry Potter* books represented rebellion against my Evangelical Christian background.

Still, *Harry Potter* books may seem relatively harmless to the music I started to listen to and the MTV music culture I endeared myself into. Whereas *Harry Potter* is in the realm of fantasy, pop music is set in real life. In fact, pop music is a part of the pop culture, which is often seen as anti-Christian in nature by many, including my parents. My parents are evidently not alone in this case. Even Evangelical colleges such as Wheaton College and Biola University discourage pop music and have forbidden dancing to their students for many years. The reason that Christian music industry is thriving is partly due to the fact that there are many Christian churches that forbid secular music and only allow listening to Christian music for its members. Although I attended public schools throughout my life, I know for a fact that there are a number of Christian schools that prohibit secular music because it represents subscription to secular culture.

To a large extent, attending public schools allowed me to explore pop music and culture without friction. In fact, most of the Christians I knew in school have. My parents, in essence, represented social dinosaurs that just simply did not understand the new contemporary world.

Nevertheless, I realize now that my parents were right. I assumed that listening to pop music was just listening to music. Yet, my parents cautioned me that pop music was not only about music but about secular culture and the secular world that stood behind the music. In my experience, I feel that they were right. I drifted from just merely hearing secular music to experiencing popular culture of which my secularized friends, many of whom were more nominal Christians, did not truly believe the Christian faith.

I would describe my life as having the theme of adversity. Some of the adversity was created by me from digressing and being defiant of my parents' teachings. The adversity that was created in my inner self from the clash of my genuine Christian faith and my desire for experiencing secular culture often created times of uncertainty and discontent. But, I would say that the adversity was not merely self-generated. In a sense, I am in true nature a baby dinosaur that belongs to its parent dinosaurs in societal terms. My parents have always raised me with much concern and care for me and my Christian growth, so that there was always an inner voice that guided me. Often, this inner voice caused problems for me because of my secularized friends who could and completely relate with me, and I struggled to find acceptance. Furthermore, the culture around me was so different than the ideal that was inculcated in my household and at the church where my father is the Senior Pastor that I found the contrast discerning many times. Still, I would say that I look positively upon from the place of my birth, Pusan, South Korea, to the present-day Closter, New Jersey because I have learned that even through my mistakes, I feel as though I am a better person today than I ever was in the sense that I feel that I know what I want from life more clearly.

.

www.ingramcontent.com/pod-product-compliance
Lightning Source LLC
Chambersburg PA
CBHW020914090426
42736CB00008B/629